JOURNEY OF

Hope

Also from the Boys Town Press

For Parents
Common Sense Parenting®
Common Sense Parenting of Toddlers and Preschoolers
Common Sense Parenting Learn-at-Home Video Kit
Angry Kids, Frustrated Parents
Parenting to Build Character in Your Teen
Dealing with Your Kids' 7 Biggest Troubles
Parents and Kids Talking about School Violence
Practical Tools for Foster Parents

For Adolescents
A Good Friend
Who's in the Mirror?
What's Right for Me?
Boundaries: A Guide for Teens

For Professionals
Teaching Social Skills to Youth
Safe and Effective Secondary Schools
The Well-Managed Classroom
The Well-Managed Classroom for Catholic Schools
The Ongoing Journey
Dangerous Kids
Building Skills in High-Risk Families

For a free Boys Town Press catalog, call
1-800-282-6657. www.girlsandboystown.org/btpress

Teens and parents who need help with any problem
can call the Girls and Boys Town National Hotline at
1-800-448-3000 anytime.

JOURNEY OF

READER

Inspirational Stories of Prophets
through the Ages

CLIFFORD STEVENS

BOYS TOWN, NEBRASKA

Journey of Hope Reader

Published by the Boys Town Press
Boys Town, Nebraska 68010

© 2001 Father Flanagan's Boys' Home

ISBN 1-889322-46-6

www.girlsandboystown.org/btpress

The Boys Town Press is the publishing division of Girls and Boys Town, the original Father Flanagan's Boys' Home.

Publisher's Cataloging-in-Publication
(Provided by Quality Books, Inc.)

Stevens, Clifford J.
    Journey of hope reader / by Clifford Stevens. -- 1st ed.
        p. cm.
    Includes bibliographical references.
    ISBN: 1-889322-46-6

    1. Christian education--Textbooks for teenagers.
2. Teenagers--Religious life. 3. Spirituality. 4. Hope--Religious aspects--Christianity. I. Title.

BV1485.S74 2001   268'.433
                                   QBI01-200255

10   9   8   7   6   5   4   3   2   1

Table of Contents

CHAPTER 1

What Is a Prophet?

O Lord, open my eyes

that I may see the need of others.

open my ears that I may hear their cries.

open my heart that they need not be without succour.

Let me be not afraid to defend the weak

because of the anger of the strong:

nor be afraid to defend the poor

because of the anger of the rich.

Show me where love and hope and faith are needed,

and use me to bring them to these places.

Open my eyes and ears that I may, this coming day,

be able to do some work of peace for Thee.

– ALAN PATON

We hold these basic principles of law and morality: We are responsible for our actions; human responsibility is at the root of human happiness and misery; good and evil are the two inter-twining threads that explain human history, as well as our own personal happiness or misery.

Each of us has a conscience, the supreme guide in moral actions. It is by listening to the voice of conscience, or not listening to it, that we determine the quality and content of our own happiness or misery.

But what about those who do not follow their conscience? What about those who are the cause of human misery because of greed, a lust for power, or simply their own convenience and comfort? Where is the conscience of human society itself, of a city, a nation, or a people? If conscience is the voice of God for the individual, who is the voice of God for society?

The Bible tells us of men and women whom God raised to be this conscience. They are prophets, the human voices of God to His people, called to make loud and clear His will in the nitty-gritty business of human affairs. These voices are as compelling today as when they were first heard two thousand five hundred years ago, and they have much to say to us in our own times. Their words are timeless, and great leaders of every age have found guidance and inspiration in their words.

When the United Nations building was being planned in New York City, the motto of this international body was taken from the prophet Isaiah and carved over the entrance to the building:

"They shall beat their swords into plowshares, and their spears into pruning hooks."

Abraham Joshua Heschel says in his book, *The Prophets,* that a prophet is one "who feels fiercely. God has thrust a burden upon his soul, and he is bowed and stunned at man's fierce greed. Frightful is the agony of man; no human voice can convey its full terror. Prophecy is the voice that God has lent to this silent agony, a voice to the plundered poor, to the profaned riches of the world. It is a form of living, a crossing point of God and man. God is raging in the prophet's words."

The prophet is the voice of the human conscience magnified for the whole human race. This voice is God's commentary on human greed, depravity, insensitivity, and injustice. It has provided a model for other prophets through the centuries who defended justice and often died for their mission.

Each of us, in a sense, is called to be a prophet in the particular circumstances of our own life and times. "The things that horrified the prophets are even now daily occurrences all over the world," says Heschel. "The sorts of crimes that filled the prophets of Israel with dismay do not go beyond that which we regard as normal ingredients of social dynamics. To us a single act of injustice – cheating in business, exploiting the poor – is minor. To the prophets, disaster. To us, injustice hurts people; to the prophets it is a deathblow to existence. To us, an episode, to them, a catastrophe, a threat to the world."

The prophets dig deep into the living flesh of humanity and cry out in pain, a cry that is the very voice of God.

HARRIET TUBMAN

Harriet Tubman was born into slavery on a plantation in Maryland, sometime around 1820. The exact date is unknown, since the birth of slaves was not recorded. As she grew up, she experienced the typical cruelties of slave life, the beatings, insults, and daily indignities. Like other slaves she became skilled in the art of passive resistance – working slowly, breaking tools, adopting a false mask of simple-minded contentment – while struggling to maintain an inner conviction that she was indeed worth more than a thing. But Tubman was not content merely to survive with her inner dignity intact. She was convinced that God intended her to be free.

It is one of the miracles of Christian history that African slaves, having received a false gospel from their "Christian" slavemasters, nevertheless heard in the biblical story a message of life and liberation. The slavemasters' catechism stressed the virtue of obedience and counseled slaves to be content with their lot. But the slaves heard a different message. The God of the Bible was the God who led Moses and the Hebrew slaves out of bondage in Egypt, who inspired the prophets, and who was incarnate in Jesus Christ. This was not the god of the slavemasters, but the God of the oppressed.

It was with this God that Harriet Tubman enjoyed a special relationship. From the time she was a child she was subject to deep trances in which she heard the voice of the Lord. In one of these visionary experiences in 1849 she saw "a line, and on the other side of that line were green fields, and lovely flowers, and beautiful white ladies, who stretched out their arms to me over the line, but I couldn't reach them no how. I always fell before I got to the line." When she awoke she took this vision as a signal for her to begin her escape.

Though small in stature, Tubman was a strong woman. She had spurned the housework coveted by most slaves in favor of backbreaking field work. She had trained herself over the years to move quietly, to be at home in nature, and to find her way in the dark. All these skills now came into play as she made her break. Traveling by night, following the North Star, she passed through swamps and forests, sleeping by day in the shelter of caves or hidden in a leafy treetop.

When she finally crossed into the free state of Pennsylvania, she looked at her hands "to see if I was the same person. There was such a glory over everything; the sun came like gold through the trees and over the fields, and I felt like I was in heaven." But at once she was seized by a sense of wider mission. "I had crossed the line. I was FREE; but there was no one to welcome me to the land of freedom. I was a stranger in a strange land; and my home, after all, was down in Maryland… But I was free and THEY should be free. I would make a home in the North and bring them there, God helping me."

And so, having made her perilous way to freedom, Tubman chose to return to the South to assist in the escape of others still in bondage. Over the next twelve years she returned a total of nineteen times to "Pharaoh's Land," in the process rescuing at least three hundred slaves, including her parents. These trips were fraught with danger at every step. It was one thing to travel alone, but quite another to move twenty or thirty people, including children, across hundreds of miles of open country. She was aided over time by a well-organized network of safe houses and supporters, the so-called Underground Railroad. After the passage of the Fugitive Slave Act in 1850 it was no longer sufficient to bring slaves to the North. Her trips extended all the way to Canada.

Though armed bounty hunters roamed the countryside, Tubman never lost a single one of her charges. A fantastic price was put on her head and wanted posters were widely circulated. Among whites she was one of the most hated figures in the South. But among slaves she was known as "Moses."

During the Civil War, Tubman worked for the Union Army, first as a nurse, then as a scout and spy. She made numerous trips behind Confederate lines. More than once, her cunning and her unassuming appearance saved her from detection. The "Moses" of the wanted posters was imagined to be a person – probably even a man – of remarkable features, certainly not a scrawny, gap-toothed old woman.

After the war Tubman retired to a small house in Auburn, New York. She was worn out and penniless, but still she devoted herself to providing shelter and care to poor blacks. She supported herself by selling vegetables from her garden. In 1869 a white admirer published *Scenes of the Life of Harriet Tubman* as a means of earning her some money. But she was used to poverty, and so she quickly dispersed her income to those in greater need. When the book was published, Frederick Douglass, the great abolitionist and himself a former slave, wrote to her:

> "Most that I have done and suffered in the service of our cause has been in public, and I have received much encouragement at every step of the way. You, on the other hand, have labored in a private way... I have had the applause of the crowd...while the most that you have done has been witnessed by a few trembling, scared, and foot-sore bondsmen and women, whom you have led out of the house of bondage, and whose heartfelt 'God bless you' has been your only reward."

Tubman lived into her nineties and died peacefully on March 10, 1913.

In what way was Harriet Tubman like the prophets in the Bible? What are some of the qualities a prophet has to have? Do you think Harriet Tubman had these qualities?

Do you believe you would have the courage to do what Harriet Tubman did? Where do you think this courage comes from?

Mouthpiece of God

Speak, Lord, for your servant hears.

Grant us ears to hear,

Eyes to see:

Will to obey,

Hearts to love,

Then declare what You will,

Reveal what You will,

Command what You will,

Demand what You will.

– CHRISTINA ROSSETTI

It is hard to gain entrance into the hearts of men and women intent on their own interests and blind to the interests of others. But this is exactly what the prophet does. The prophet proclaims that God is preoccupied with human beings and the actual events of history, rather than with the unchanging self-serving aims of politicians. Because human beings are so cherished by God, the tiniest injustices concern Him. And He makes the prophet His mouthpiece.

Prophets use emotional, poetic language and fierce, fiery images, announced with a sense of urgency. That is why the prophet is often condemned, cast out, and rejected. Those involved in injustices that cause suffering to others are often not willing to face the wrath of God in the words and actions of the prophet.

It is a sad fact of human life that sensitivity to evil often overwhelms sensitivity to good. We can often mouth statements about compassion and kindness while people are starving and misused almost on our doorstep. Religion and morality are often more on one's lips than in one's personal behavior …and this is what the prophet lashes out against.

The prophets proclaim that God is concerned about the suffering of the poor, the cries of the oppressed, the hunger of children, the sorrow of the bereaved, the abandonment of orphans. The prophet is the voice of God's concern, which embraces every form of human suffering and injustice.

The prophet makes us examine our own conduct, our own greed, our own lack of compassion, and our own insensitivity to the welfare of our fellow human beings. The story of Lazarus and the rich man in the Gospel is a prophetic message from Jesus himself. The rich man thinks only of himself and not the starving beggar at the door. He is intent only upon his own prosperity and has no eye for the suffering of others. Jesus indicates that that kind of insensitivity ends, not in a blessed Eternity, but in eternal anguish. God is the defender of the poor, the homeless, the hungry, and the suffering.

Look at yourself, and look around you: Do you have any true concern about the feelings of those you live with? Do you keep your eye open for saying the good word that will cheer and encourage, or for doing the good deed that will bring a smile to someone's face and warmth to his or her heart?

If a prophet were to look at your life, what would he or she say? What is not in keeping with the compassion of God? How do you love and treat your neighbor as yourself? When have you done something to another that you would not want to have done to you? When have you been so preoccupied with your own convenience and comfort that you did not notice the discomfort or inconvenience of others? When was the last time you shared something of your own with someone else?

BARTOLOMÉ DE LAS CASAS

Bartolomé de Las Casas was the most distinguished of a number of Dominican friars who raised their voices against the rapacious violence inflicted on the Indians of the Americas. Las Casas was not content to denounce the excesses of the Conquest. Reading the gospel from the perspective of what he called "the scourged Christ of the Indies," he articulated a theological understanding of religious freedom, human rights, and the relation between salvation and social justice, that was scarcely matched again in the Catholic church before the Second Vatican Council. Five hundred years after the collision of cultures in the Americas, Las Casas is chiefly recognized as a prophet, who anticipated by many centuries the church's "preferential option for the poor."

As a boy of eight, Las Casas witnessed the return of Columbus to Seville after his first voyage to the New World. He made his own first trip to Hispaniola in 1502. After studies in Rome for the priesthood he returned to the New World, where he served as chaplain in the Spanish conquest of Cuba. Though a priest, he also benefited from the Conquest as the owner of an *encomienda,* a plantation with Indian indentured laborers.

In 1514 however, he underwent a dramatic conversion, prompted by his witnessing the genocidal cruelty inflicted on the Indians. He soon joined the Dominican order and became a passionate and prophetic defender of the indigenous peoples. For more than fifty years he traveled back and forth between the New World and the court of Spain, attempting through his books, letters, and preaching to expose the cruelties of the Conquest, whose very legitimacy, and not merely excesses, he disavowed.

Although the main attraction for the Spanish in the New World was gold, the Conquest was ostensibly justified by evangelical motivations. The pope had authorized the subjugation of the Indian populations for the purpose of implanting the gospel and securing their salvation. Las Casas claimed that the deeds of the conquistadors revealed their true religion:

> "In order to gild a very cruel and harsh tyranny that destroys so many villages and people, solely for the sake of satisfying the greed of men and giving them gold, the latter, who themselves do not know the faith, use the pretext of teaching it to others and thereby deliver up the innocent in order to extract from their blood *the wealth which these men regard as their god.*"

Las Casas vehemently opposed the notion that the gospel could be spread through slaughter or compulsion of any kind. While others claimed that the Indians were a lesser race, he affirmed their full humanity, and thus their entitlement to all human rights. For his writings on human equality and his defense of the right to religious freedom, Las Casas deserves to be remembered as a political philosopher of extreme significance in the history of ideas.

But Las Casas's theological insights went far beyond a simple affirmation of the Indians' human dignity. Identifying the Indians with the poor, in the gospel sense, he argued that in their sufferings they represented the crucified Christ. He wrote, "I leave in the Indies Jesus Christ, our God, scourged and afflicted and beaten and crucified not once, but thousands of times."

For Las Casas there could be no salvation in Jesus Christ apart from social justice. Thus, the question was not whether the Indians were to be "saved"; the more serious question was the salvation of the Spanish who were persecuting Christ in his poor.

In 1543, with court officials in Spain eager to be rid of him, Las Casas was named bishop of the impoverished region of Chiapas in southern Mexico. There he immediately alienated his flock by refusing absolution to any Spaniard who would not free his Indian slaves. He was denounced to the Spanish court as a "lunatic" and received numerous death threats. Eventually he resigned his bishopric and returned to Spain, where he felt he could more effectively prosecute his cause. There he died on July 18, 1566, at the age of eighty-two.

Was Las Casas a prophet? How? What do you think motivated Las Casas to defend the Native Americans?

The prophet applies the judgment of God to personal human affairs, not to earth-shaking events or political issues, but to the child who has nothing to eat, the homeless man who cannot defend himself, the kid in the next neighborhood who is different from you, the man with an accent in the grocery store, to anyone who is in need.

The work of the prophet is to make us all partners of God through our compassion and sensitivity to others. It is so easy to claim that we worship God and are devoted to Him, yet never show it in our actions. Like the man who found a beggar in rags sleeping in front of the store he was entering: "And you know," the man said afterwards, "when I came out of the store, he was still lying there on the street. No one had helped him!" Why didn't he help him?

The prophets try to convince us that we get the bulk of our happiness *from making others happy.* Few people really believe that. Most people try to get their happiness at the expense of others' happiness, or by building on others' disadvantages. For most of us, it is very difficult, if not impossible, to change direction.

The prophet always begins with a message of doom and ends with a message of hope. The prophet is not someone who *predicts,* but *warns* that something will happen. The mission is to declare the word of God here and now, not in the future. The prophet emphasizes the critical importance of goodwill toward each other, the true meaning of guilt, and the power of sin to corrupt and destroy the bonds that link one person with another.

CHAPTER 2

Conscience of a Nation

Here I am, Lord.

Here is my body,

Here is my heart,

Here is my soul.

Grant that I may be big enough to reach the world,

Strong enough to carry it.

Pure enough to embrace it without wanting to keep it.

Grant that I may be a meeting-place, but a temporary
　　　one,

A road that does not end in itself,

Because everything to be gathered there, everything
　　　human,

Leads towards You.

– MICHEL QUOIST

We all get ourselves into trouble; we do not listen to good advice; we often think we know it all, and we are sure that we can be masters of our own destiny. We all have the voice of conscience inside us, yet we can ignore it for many reasons. Then, we blame everyone else for our own misery.

Isaiah had the difficult job of being the conscience of a whole nation, of kings and commoners, of army generals and farmers. He carried on that mission for over forty years. But no one listened to him. The people of Judah had been chosen by God to be His special people, but they constantly deserted Him for other gods or personal advantage.

Isaiah was called to be a prophet at a time of great prosperity, but it was this very prosperity that was the great threat. The long reign of King Uzziah lasted forty-one years. He built up the economy of the country, strengthened the military, and commanded at least three successful wars against the Philistines, the Arabians, and the Ammonites. He was a superb administrator, whose kingdom prospered during his reign.

It was in the year 742 B.C. when Uzziah died, that Isaiah received his calling. The powerful kingdom of Judah was declining, and a great threat was rising in the north: the Assyrian empire. In their prosperity, the people of Judah had turned away from God. It was not the power of Assyria that posed the real threat to Judah; it was the people's infidelity.

> The ox knows its owner, and the donkey its master's
> crib,
> Israel does not know; my people do not understand.

The whole head is sick, the whole heart is diseased.

From the sole of the foot to the head there is nothing
    healthy,

Only wounds, bruises, open sores,

Not dressed, not bandaged, not soothed with ointment.

Your country is desolate.

– ISAIAH 1:3-6

Isaiah told them: You are not in danger from anything if you follow your conscience and remain faithful to your God. The danger was not from without; it was from within.

But they would listen to no one. Then disaster threatened. The Assyrian empire started to take over the smaller countries surrounding it. "What will happen to us?" was on everyone's lips, and the king was concerned. Isaiah's mission was to convince the king and his people that their security was in God, that they were the chosen people of God, who would defend them in every danger, as long as they remained faithful to their covenant.

Come, let us talk this over, says the Lord.

Though your sins be as scarlet,

They shall be as white as snow.

Though they be crimson red,

They shall be white as wool.

If you are willing, and obey,

You shall eat the good things of the land.

– ISAIAH 1:18-19

17

Conscience alone is the secure guide. It is only by following one's conscience that happiness is to be found, because happiness comes from the blessing of God. It is a hard lesson to learn. We have all made the mistake of not following our conscience at times. How often have you made that mistake? What were the consequences?

FANNIE LOU HAMER

Fannie Lou Hamer was born the daughter of sharecroppers in the Mississippi Delta, a poor black woman in the poorest region of America. And yet she rose up from obscurity to challenge the mighty rulers of her day, a towering prophet whose eloquence and courage helped guide and inspire the struggle for freedom.

Until 1962 her life was little different from other poor black women in rural Mississippi. One of twenty children in her family, she was educated to the fourth grade and, like her parents before her, fell into the life of sharecropping. This system allowed poor farmers to work a piece of the plantation owner's land in exchange for payment of a share of their crop. In practice, it was a system of debt slavery that combined with segregation and brute force to keep the black population poor and powerless. Looking back on her own twenty years of sharecropping, Hamer later said, "Sometimes I be working in the fields and I get so tired, I say to the people picking cotton with us, 'Hard as we have to work for nothing, there must be some way we can change this.'"

The way opened for Hamer when she attended a civil rights rally in 1962 and heard a preacher issue a call for blacks to register to vote. At the age of forty-five Hamer answered the call, though it meant overcoming numerous threats and obstacles and resulted in the eviction of her family from their plantation home. She took this as a sign to commit herself to full-time work for the freedom movement, serving as a field secretary for the Student Nonviolent Coordinating Committee, and quickly, rising to a position of leadership.

For a black person in 1963 to challenge the system of segregation in Mississippi was literally to court death. Hamer, like other activists in the movement, faced this reality on a daily basis. In the summer of 1963 she was part of a group arrested in Charleston, South Carolina, after they illegally entered the side of a bus terminal reserved for whites. While in jail she was savagely beaten, emerging with a damaged kidney and her eyesight permanently impaired.

In 1964, Hamer led a "Freedom Delegation" from Mississippi to the National Convention of the Democratic Party in Atlantic City. There they tried unsuccessfully to challenge the credentials of the official white delegation. President Lyndon Johnson would tolerate no embarrassment to the party bosses of the South, and the Freedom Delegation was evicted. But Hamer touched the conscience of the nation with her eloquent account of the oppression of blacks in the segregated South and the nonviolent struggle to affirm their dignity and their rights.

In later years, Hamer's concern grew beyond civil rights to include early opposition to the Vietnam War

and efforts to forge a coalition among all poor and working people of America – the Poor People's Campaign
that Martin Luther King left uncompleted. In all these
endeavors, Hamer was sustained by her deep biblical
faith in the God of the oppressed.

"We have to realize," she once observed, "just how
grave the problem is in the United States today, and I
think the sixth chapter of Ephesians, the eleventh and
twelfth verses help us to know...what it is we are up
against. It says, 'Put on the whole armor of God, that ye
may be able to stand against the wiles of the devil. For
we wrestle not against flesh and blood but against prin-
cipalities, against powers, against the rulers of the darkness of this world, against spiritual wickedness in high
places.' This is what I think about when I think of my
own work in the fight for freedom."

In the nonviolent struggle of the 1960s ordinary people – men, women and children – became saints and
prophets. Inspired by a vision of justice and freedom,
sustained by faith, they found the strength to confront
their fears and stand up to dogs, fire hoses, clubs, and
bombs. In the ranks of this extraordinary movement
Hamer was a rock who did as much as anyone of her
time to redeem the promise of the gospel and the ideals
of America. She said,

> "Christianity is being concerned about your fel-
> low man, not building a million-dollar church
> while people are starving right around the corner.
> Christ was a revolutionary person, out there

where it was happening. That's what God is all about, and that's where I get my strength."

Hamer died of breast cancer on March 14, 1977.

Do you agree with Hamer's definition of Christianity? How did she live up to that definition? Can you think of ways you can show concern for your fellow human beings?

CHIEF SEATTLE OF THE SUQUAMISH

Seattle was born in a Suquamish village along the Puget Sound, sometime around 1786. As a child he witnessed the arrival of the first whites in the Northwest. They were trappers and traders who did not come to stay. But for Seattle and his people, it was the beginning of irrevocable change.

In his early twenties Seattle was named the chief of his tribe. By this time the early white visitors had opened the way for an ever-increasing stream of settlers. It fell to Seattle to set a strategy for dealing with these invaders with their insatiable claims. Seattle rejected the option of violent resistance and put his trust in the possibilities of peaceful dialogue. But as the full intentions of the whites became clear, his goal was reduced simply to ensuring the survival of his people.

In 1830 Seattle and many of the Indians of Puget Sound converted to Christianity. As a leader of his people he tried to integrate the principals of his faith with the beliefs of his ancestors. But with each passing year, it seemed that his traditional world was getting smaller. Ultimately, Seattle came to believe that the struggle with the whites really represented the contrast between spiritual values. In particular the Indians and the whites held to completely different understandings of the relationship between human beings and the earth.

The whites considered the land something to be bought and sold. As Seattle observed, "How can you buy or sell the sky, the warmth of the land? The idea is strange to us… Every part of this earth is sacred to my people. Every shining pine needle, every sandy shore, every mist in the dark woods, every clearing and humming insect is holy in the memory and experience of my people… We are part of the earth and it is part of us."

In 1855, Seattle signed the Port Elliott Treaty, which transferred ancestral Indian lands to the federal government and established a reservation for Native American tribes in the Northwest region. The alternative, he believed, was the extinction of his people. But he took the opportunity to address a letter to President Franklin Pierce. It is a haunting and prophetic document, often cited today by the proponents of ecology. It certainly does reflect Seattle's profound ecological imagination, as well as the spiritual vision in which it was rooted:

"We know that the White Man does not understand our ways. One portion of the land is the same to him as the next, for he is a stranger who comes in the night and takes from the land whatever he needs. The earth is not his brother, but his enemy, and when he has conquered it, he moves on.

"One thing we know, which the White Man may one day discover – our God is the same God. You may think now that you own Him as you wish to own our land; but you cannot. He is the God of humanity, and his compassion is equal for the red man and the white. The earth is precious to him, and to harm the earth is to heap contempt on the Creator… Even the white man cannot be exempt from the common destiny. We may be brothers after all. We shall see."

Chief Seattle died on June 7, 1866, on the Port Madison Reservation near the city which today bears his name.

Do you think Chief Seattle's words were prophetic? Explain.

Pain of a Prophet

O Ineffable Lord,

God of the Ages,

Whose name remains unspoken,

Who enfolds us in our living and our dying

With mystic threads that link us

With the flaming Seraphim,

Immortal and undying.

Help us to glimpse,

In this our little while,

Some gleam from that bright moment,

As we ponder now and wait the coming dawn.

– CLIFFORD STEVENS

God is not only Creator and Lord, Almighty and Immortal, the King of the Ages and the Master of the Universe. He is also a kind, gracious, loving Father, who is saddened at the sufferings and misfortunes of His children.

Isaiah speaks to all of us when he cries out to the people of Judah about God's sadness at the infidelity of His people, who have turned away from Him and no longer call upon His name:

> The faithful city,
> What has she become?
> Justice used to dwell in her,
> But now assassins!
> Your silver has turned to dust,
> Your wine is mixed with water.
> Your princes are rebels,
> Companions of thieves.
>
> For now the Sovereign, the Lord of Hosts,
> Is taking away from Jerusalem and from Judah
> Support and staff,
> No bread, no water,
> No warrior, no soldier,
> No judge, no prophet,
>
> For Jerusalem has stumbled and Judah has fallen,
> Because their speech and their deeds are against
>   the Lord,
> Defying His glorious presence!
>
> – ISAIAH 1:21-23

It is a fearful thing to turn one's back on God, but that is what His people had done.

In 735 B.C., Uzziah's son, Ahaz, became king of Judah, and he found himself in a political crisis. The Assyrian empire, with its capital at Damascus, was spreading terror through the whole region, conquering its neighbors and threatening rulers in every kingdom. Judah's neighboring kings had worked together to throw off the Assyrian threat. They asked Ahaz to join them.

Ahaz refused and found himself and his kingdom under siege from the neighboring kings. Jerusalem was in a state of panic. There seemed only one way to save Jerusalem: appeal to the king of Assyria.

To Isaiah, this was the greatest kind of abandonment: not to turn to the Lord in prayer and fasting or to the keeping of His covenant. For Isaiah, this was a formula for even greater disaster.

"You have made a covenant with death," he told the people of Judah, "an agreement with Hell...and it will not hold. Your men will fall by the sword, your warriors in battle, and her gates will moan and mourn. She will sit on the ground, deserted." (Isaiah 28:18, 3:25-26)

In a last cry of pain, Isaiah cried out, "Let me sing to my friend a song of his love for his vineyard. Turn to God as Father and Friend. Though your sins be as scarlet, they shall be as white as snow, though they be crimson red, they shall be spotless as wool."

Do you see God as Father and friend? Why or why not? Have you behaved at times like the people of Judah? How can you find your way back? What of Isaiah's message applies to us today?

THE SLEEPING SENTINEL

On a rainy morning in September 1861, during the first year of the Civil War, a group of Union soldiers came to the White House to plead for the life of one of their friends. They were granted an audience with President Lincoln himself, and in faltering words they told why they had come.

The soldiers were part of the 3rd Vermont Regiment, which was made up of mostly farm boys from the Green Mountains. Since their arrival in Washington they had been stationed at Chain Bridge, a few miles above the city. The bridge was of vital importance since Confederate forces occupied the hills on the opposite side of the Potomac River. The soldiers' orders were strict: Any sentinel caught sleeping at his post was to be shot within twenty-four hours.

According to the soldiers' story, a boy named William Scott had enlisted in Company K. He had been on duty one night, and the following night had taken the place of a comrade too sick to stand guard. The third night he had been called out on guard duty yet again. The young fellow could not keep awake for three nights in a row. When the relief guard came around, he was found asleep. Arrested, tried, and found guilty, he was sentenced to be shot.

"William Scott, sir, is as brave a soldier as there is in your army," the Green Mountain Boys told Lincoln. "He is no coward. It's not right to shoot him like a traitor and bury him like a dog."

Later in the day President Lincoln rode from the White House in the direction of Chain Bridge. Within a day or so the newspapers reported that a soldier sentenced to death for sleeping at his post had been pardoned by the president, and had returned to his regiment.

It was a long time before Scott would speak of his interview with President Lincoln. One day he told a comrade the whole story.

"I knew the president at once," he said, "by a Lincoln medal I had long worn. I was scared at first, for I had never talked with a great man before. He asked me all about the folks at home, my brothers and sisters, and where I went to school, and how I liked it. Then he asked me about my mother. I showed him her picture. He said if he were in my place he would try to make a fond mother happy, and never cause her a sorrow or a tear.

""My boy,' he said, 'you are not going to be shot. You are going back to your regiment. I have been put to a good deal of trouble on your account. Now what I want to know is how you are going to pay me back. My bill is a large one, and there is only one man in all the world who can pay it. His name is William Scott. If from this day you will promise to do your whole duty as a soldier, then the debt will be paid. Will you make that promise and try to keep it?' "

Gladly the young Vermont soldier made the promise, and well did he keep it. From that day William Scott became a model man of his regiment. He was never absent from a roll call. He was always on hand if there was any hard work to do. He worked nights in the hospital, nursing the sick and wounded, because it trained him to keep awake. He made a record for himself on picket duty, and distinguished himself as a scout.

Sometime after this the 3rd Vermont went into one of its many hard battles. They were ordered to attack the Confederate lines, and William Scott fell in the enemy volley.

His comrades caught him up, carried him bleeding and dying from the field, and laid him on a cot.

"Tell the president I have tried to be a good soldier, and true to the flag," he said.

Then, making a last effort, with his dying breath he prayed for Abraham Lincoln.

Company K buried William Scott in a grove just in the rear of the camp, at the foot of a big oak tree. Deep into the oak they cut the initials "W.S." and under it the words "A Brave Soldier."

Why do you think President Lincoln pardoned William Scott? What did he require of Scott in return? How did Scott demonstrate his faithfulness after Lincoln's pardon? In what ways can you demonstrate fidelity to God?

JOHN HOWARD GRIFFIN

In 1959, John Howard Griffin traveled to New Orleans. There, with the help of drugs, dyes, and radiation, he darkened his skin, shaved his head, and "crossed the line into a country of hate, fear, and hopelessness – the country of the American Negro." For two months he traveled through the Deep South, later publishing his observations in a magazine series and the widely acclaimed book *Black Like Me*. Griffin's effort to cross the color line was the most dramatic gesture in a life devoted to radical empathy. But for Griffin it was simply another exploration of the concern that preoccupied him throughout his life – the struggle to discover what it means, finally, to be a human being.

Born in Texas on June 16, 1920, Griffin was educated in France, where he studied medicine and music until the outbreak of World War II. After the German occupation he helped run a network smuggling Jews out of the country and narrowly escaped arrest by the Gestapo. He spent most of the war in military service in the South Pacific. Toward the end of the war a nearby explosion impaired his vision and eventually left him completely blind.

The experience of blindness and severe illnesses that visited him throughout his life imposed a stark choice – either to give in to despair or to trust in some higher purpose. "Tragedy," he wrote, "is not in the condition but in man's perception of the condition." Despite his handicap, Griffin went on to study music, married and raised a family, tried his hand at ranching, and wrote two novels.

Then in 1957 something miraculous happened. A blockage of circulation to the optic nerve suddenly opened, restoring his sight. He saw his wife and two young children for the first time. For some years he had been studying theology, and in his journal he described the joy he felt in being able to read the Divine Office: "The soul's nourishment, the soul's normalcy, sinking beyond the words to their innermost meaning, seeking and thirsting for it... This morning, then, the tired brain, the battered brain conceived the idea of reading the clear black type of the Office. And therein found full reason and justification for seeing again."

With the return of his sight Griffin became aware of how much we do not see, of the way superficial obstacles can serve as obstacles to true perception – especially in the illusion that allows us to regard our fellow humans as "the intrinsic other." Nowhere did this seem so true as in the case of American racism. Yet Griffin was struck by the frequent challenge from black friends: "The only way you can know what it's like is to wake up with my skin." He took these words to heart. The result was the journey recorded in *Black Like Me.*

The book received and sustained enormous attention, though not all readers recognized it as a deeply spiritual work. Griffin's concerns went beyond a set of social conditions to the underlying disease of the soul. His book was really a meditation on the effects of dehumanization, both for the persecuted and the persecutors themselves. As he described it, he had changed nothing but the color of his skin – and yet that was everything. He discovered the hateful face that white Americans reserved for blacks; it was a devastating experience. "Future historians," he wrote later, "will be mystified that generations of us could stand in the midst of this sickness and never see it, never really feel how our System distorted and dwarfed human lives because these lives happened to inhabit bodies encased in a darker skin; and how, in cooperating with this System, it distorted and dwarfed our own lives in a subtle and terrible way."

After his story was published, Griffin was exposed to a more personal form of hostility. His body was hung in effigy in the main street of his town. His life was repeatedly threatened. Nevertheless he threw himself into a decade of tireless work on behalf of the growing civil rights movement. Necessity forced him, much against his nature, into the role of activist. "One hopes," he wrote, "that if one acts from a thirst for justice and suffers the consequences, then others who share one's thirst may be spared the terror of disesteem and persecution." And so he persevered with those who shared "the harsh and terrible understanding that somehow they must pit the quality of their love against the quantity of hate roaming the world."

For years Griffin suffered from a range of afflictions, some possibly induced by the skin treatments he had undergone years before. He died (of "everything," according to his wife) on September 8, 1980.

What finally was the meaning of his life? "The world," he once wrote, "has always been saved by an Abrahamic minority… There have always been a few who, in times of great trouble, became keenly aware of the underlying tragedy: the needless destruction of humanity."

Explain how Griffin's book, Black Like Me, *awakened people to racial injustice and suffering. Do you think John Griffin was a prophet? Explain.*

CHAPTER 4

God's Promise of Hope and Healing

Almighty God,

In whom we live and move and have our being,

You have made us for Yourself

So that our hearts are restless until they rest in Thee.

Grant us purity of heart and strength of purpose,

That no passion may hinder us from knowing Your will,

No weakness from doing it;

But in Your light may we see light clearly,

And in Your service find perfect freedom.

– ST. AUGUSTINE OF HIPPO

Do you know who you are and where you are going? How could you, unless you consult the One Who made you? If you picked up a violin before violins were invented or stood before a computer before you knew what it was, you would have no idea what it was made for. You are more than blood and bones, muscles and sinews, eyes, ears, throat, and stomach. You have to know where you came from and where you are going if you are to make any sense out of who you are.

The same was true of the Jewish people at the time of Isaiah. When they became prosperous, they forgot God and their covenant with Him. And when they were in trouble, they did not look for help from God, but from the political power and military might of the kingdom of Assyria. Judah became the vassal of Assyria and lost its independence, exactly as Isaiah warned. He told the people of Judah that terrible things would happen to them for deserting their God, but there was more to his message:

> It will happen in days to come
> that the mountain of God's house
> will rise higher than the mountains round about,
> and tower above the highest peaks.
> Then all nations will stream to it,
> many peoples will come to it and say,
> "Come, let us go up to the mountain of the Lord,
> to the house of the God of Jacob.
> that He may teach us His ways,
> so that we may walk in His paths."
> For the law will issue from Zion,
> and the word of the Lord from Jerusalem.
>
> They will hammer their swords into plowshares,
> and their spears into sickles.

Nation shall not lift sword against nation,

no longer will they learn how to make war.

House of Jacob, come, let us walk in the Lord's light.

– ISAIAH 2:2-4

God's punishment does not last forever, but His blessing is dependent on us to change our ways and walk in the way of His commandments. Disaster comes from placing our security and happiness in other people and things. What is being revealed when God forgives us is His tenderness and mercy, His undying love and enduring kindness. There is even a phrase from St. Francis of Assisi which says that *la cortesia e una della proprietate di Dio: courtesy is a quality of God.* It is not only a quality, but a property, as speech and laughter are properties of human beings.

Our conscience is our personal, inborn prophet that reminds us again and again what is right and what is wrong. When we refuse to listen to *our* personal prophet, we, too, face disaster. But Isaiah's words to the people of Israel about God's tenderness and courtesy apply to us as well. We, too, are urged, "let us walk in the Lord's light."

DIAMONDS AND TOADS

Once upon a time there was a woman who had two daughters. The elder daughter was very much like her mother in face and manner. They were both so disagreeable and so proud that there was no living with them.

The younger daughter was like her father, for she was good and sweet-tempered, and very beautiful. As people naturally love their own likeness, the mother was very fond of her elder daughter, and at the same time had a great dislike for the younger. She made her eat in the kitchen and work all the time.

Among other things, this poor child was obliged to go twice a day to draw a pitcherful of water from the spring in the woods, two miles from the house.

One day, when she reached the spring, a poor woman came to her and begged her for a drink.

"Oh, yes! With all my heart, ma'am," said this pretty little girl, and she took some clear, cool water from the spring, and held up the pitcher so that the woman might drink easily.

When she had finished, the woman said, "You are so very pretty, my dear, so good and so kind, that I cannot help giving you a gift."

Now this was a fairy, who had taken the form of a poor country woman to see how this pretty girl would treat her. "I will give you for a gift," continued the fairy, "that at every word you speak, either a flower or a jewel shall come out of your mouth."

When the girl reached home, her mother scolded her for staying so long at the spring. "I beg your pardon, Mamma," said the poor girl, "for not making more haste." And as she spoke, there came out of her mouth two roses, two pearls, and two large diamonds.

"What is it I see there?" said the mother, very much surprised. "I think I see pearls and diamonds come out of the girl's mouth! How does this happen, my child?"

This was the first time she had ever called her "my child," or spoken kindly to her.

The poor child told her mother all that had happened at the spring, and of the old woman's promise. All the time jewels and flowers fell from her lips.

"This is delightful," cried the mother. "I must send my dearest child to the spring. Come, Fanny, see what comes out of your sister's mouth when she speaks! Would you not be glad, my dear, to have the same gift given to you? All you will have to do is to take the pitcher to the spring in the wood. When a poor woman asks you for a drink, give it to her."

"It would be a fine thing for me to do," said the selfish girl. "I will not go to draw water! The child can give me her jewels. She does not need them."

"Yes, you shall," said the mother, "and you shall go this minute."

At last the elder daughter went, grumbling and scolding all the way, and taking with her the best silver pitcher in the house.

She had no sooner reached the spring than she saw a beautiful lady coming out of the wood, who came up to her and asked her for a drink. This was, you must know, the same fairy who had met her sister, but who had now taken the form of a princess.

"I did not come out here to serve you with water," said the proud, selfish maid. "Do you think I brought this silver pitcher so far just to give you a drink? You can draw water from the spring as well as I."

"You are not very polite," said the fairy. "Since you are so rude and so unkind, I give you for a gift that at every word you speak, toads and serpents shall come out of your mouth."

As soon as the mother saw her daughter coming, she cried out, "Well, my dear, did you see the good fairy?"

"Yes, Mother," answered the proud girl, and as she spoke, two serpents and two toads fell from her mouth.

"What is this that I see?" cried the mother. "What have you done?"

The girl tried to answer, but at every word toads and serpents came from her lips.

And so it was forever after. Jewels and flowers fell from the lips of the younger daughter, who was so good and kind, but the elder daughter could not speak without a shower of serpents and toads.

There is a prophecy in this story. What is it? What does it say to you about the value of kindness, courtesy, and good manners?

ARTHUR ASHE

The rise of Arthur Ashe in tennis, crowned by his Wimbledon victory in 1975, took on the stature of a fable. He was a black man in a sport that seemed a metaphor for racism – a sport played by white people in white clothes at white country clubs – and for a time he was the best there was. He was also a rare champion who believed that personal success imposes broad responsibilities to humanity.

Mr. Ashe's life was linked to two of the great social scourges of his day: racism and AIDS, the disease that led to his death. He confronted them head-on – driven, until the end, by the unselfish and unswerving conviction that he was duty-bound to ease the lives of others who were similarly afflicted.

In 1970, he began a public campaign against apartheid, seeking a visa to play in the South African Open. Three years later he won that fight and became the first black man ever to reach the final of the open. His appearance inspired young South African blacks, among them the writer and former tennis player Mark Mathabane. In his memoir, *Kafir Boy,* Mr. Mathabane wrote that the more he learned about Arthur Ashe the more he dreamed of freedom:

"What if I, too, were someday to attain the same fame and fortune as Arthur Ashe?" Mr. Mathabane wrote. "Would whites respect me as they did him? Would I be as free as he?" That dream came true when Mr. Mathabane won a tennis scholarship and immigrated to America.

Arthur Ashe took his crusade to America's inner cities as well, where he established tennis clinics and preached tennis discipline and provided hope to the young people who most needed it.

He contracted AIDS through a transfusion of tainted blood during heart-bypass surgery. He learned of his infection in 1988, but did not disclose it until 1992, after *USA Today* told him it planned to publish an article about his illness. After his public admission, Mr. Ashe campaigned vigorously on behalf of AIDS sufferers and started a foundation to combat the disease.

Arthur Ashe did not waste his fame; he used it to leave a mark on the social canvas of his time. For this he remains a model champion.

Describe how Arthur Ashe fought racism. Who regarded Ashe as a prophet? How did he use his fame to help others?

President Abraham Lincoln delivered the following address on November 19,1863, at Gettysburg, Pennsylvania, site of a major Union Army victory.

LINCOLN'S GETTYSBURG ADDRESS

Four score and seven years ago, our fathers brought forth on this continent, a new nation, conceived in Liberty, and dedicated to the proposition that all men are created equal.

Now are we engaged in a great civil war, testing whether that nation, or any nation so conceived and so dedicated, can long endure. We are met on a great battlefield of that war. We have come to dedicate a portion of that field, as a final resting place for those who here gave their lives that that nation might live. It is altogether fitting and proper that we should do this.

But, in a larger sense, we can not dedicate, we can not consecrate, we can not hallow this ground. The brave men, living and dead, who struggled here, have consecrated it, far above our poor power to add or detract.

The world will little note, nor long remember what we say here, but it can never forget what they did here. It is for us the living, rather, to be dedicated here to the unfinished work which they who fought here have thus far so nobly advanced. It is rather for us to be here dedicated to the great task remaining before us – that from these honored dead we take increased devotion to that cause for which they gave the last full measure of devotion – that we here highly resolve that these dead shall not have died in vain – that this nation, under God, shall have a new birth of freedom – and that government of the people, by the people, for the people, shall not perish from the earth.

There is a prophecy in Lincoln's Gettysburg Address. What is it? What does it promise? What qualities do you see in those men who "gave the last full measure of devotion"? Why is Abraham Lincoln considered our most "prophetic" president?

The Voice of God

Lord, I'm so glad

We don't have to be creative geniuses

Or serve elegant gourmet meals

To make our guests feel warm and wanted.

We need rather to expose them to love

And introduce them to laughter.

We need to listen and never drown them out.

Above all, we need to remember

That there is no substitute –

None whatever –

For concentrated sharing

And genuine caring.

– RUTH HARMS CALKIN

Listening to the voice of conscience is not an easy thing to do. Sometimes it is drowned out by louder voices, immersion in jobs and social activities, or just plain stupidity. Our conscience screams when we know we are doing something wrong, but we can turn the scream off or pay no attention to it. Our conscience can be our own personal prophet – the voice of God.

Jeremiah was the conscience of the kingdom of Judah two hundred years after Isaiah, but no one would listen to him, either. Judah was under siege from the kingdom of Babylonia under its king, Nebuchadnezzar, who had conquered the kingdom of Assyria. It was the sad duty of Jeremiah to tell the king and his people that disaster was upon them. They were to be conquered and taken into captivity by the king of Babylonia. Their exile from their native land would last a long time.

Terrible things were to happen. Jerusalem would be invaded and captured, the temple would be burned, and everyone would be deported to Babylon. During all this time, Jeremiah was in the city prophesying what would happen. The king and his subjects considered him a thorn in their sides, and a traitor. One time they threw him into a cistern to keep him quiet.

THE MAN WHO MOVED THE EARTH

It began with mathematics. At age twenty-one, Nicolaus Copernicus (1473-1543) was dazzling the learned men of the University of Cracow with his extraordinary abilities. In fact, the college had grown a bit boastful of its star student, and whenever visiting dignitaries arrived, young Copernicus was given chalk and blackboard and put through the paces. He could work out problems involving a dozen figures and many fractions with a directness and precision that made him a wonder in that part of the world.

A college professor traveling through Poland invited the young genius to come to Italy with him and teach mathematics. Copernicus accepted and traveled to Bologna. There he heard a series of lectures on astronomy – lectures that changed not only his life, but how men regarded their universe. For as Copernicus listened, his heart beat fast. At once he perceived how mathematics could be made valuable in calculating the movements of the stars.

For fourteen centuries, the best astronomers had based all of their science on the great book *The Almagest,* written by Ptolemy. It taught that the earth was the center of the universe, and that the sun and stars moved around it. To this theory, priests and astrologers gradually added their own explanations of the heavens. Most assumed that the earth was flat and had four corners. The stars were jewels hung in the sky and were moved about by angels. An angel looked after each star as well as all persons who were born under that star's influence, or else appointed some other angel for the purpose. Every person had a guardian angel to protect him from the evil spirits that occasionally broke out of Hell and came up to earth to tempt men.

In talking to astronomers, Copernicus perceived that very seldom did they know anything of mathematics. This ignorance on their part caused him to doubt them entirely. He sat up all night in the belfry of the cathedral and watched the stars. They moved steadily, surely, and without caprice. It was all natural, and could be reduced, Copernicus thought, to a mathematical system.

And so he began to study the matter. As he wondered and pondered, the truth began to dawn on him: The universe does not revolve around the earth. Indeed, the earth is a globe *revolving around the sun.* Like the other planets, it too is a heavenly body.

He began to teach what he was learning. In his lectures he made various references to Columbus's recent voyage, mentioning the obvious fact that in sailing westward he did not fall over the edge of the world into Hell itself, as it had been prophesied he would. He also explained that the red sky at sunset was not caused by reflections from Hell, nor was the sun moved behind a mountain by giant angels at night. He pointed out that to a man on a boat, the shore seemed to be moving past; could not the seeming movements of the stars likewise be caused by the moving of the earth?

Then, one day, a cardinal came from the Vatican to visit the young mathematician. In all kindness he cautioned him, and in love explained to him it was all right for a man to believe what he wished, but to teach others things that were not authorized was a mistake.

Copernicus was abashed. He was a deeply religious man. He only wanted to help men find the truth and understand the laws of God. He had thought his new ideas would add to the knowledge of Creation, and the beauty of the Church as well. It crushed him now to hear the rumors circulating – that he was trying to

"dethrone God by a tape measure and a yardstick."
Certain priests publicly denounced him. They declared
he was guilty of heresy and accused him of stating
things he could not prove. "You would have us believe
the earth wobbles around the sun, like a moth around a
lamp!" they sneered. "Outrageous!"

And so Copernicus packed his bags and went back to
Poland. There he became a canon of the cathedral in the
sleepy town of Frauenburg. And there he was a watched
man. He lived in practical isolation and exile, for the
Church had forbidden him to speak publicly on unauthorized themes. The universities and prominent
churchmen were ordered to leave Copernicus and his
theories alone.

Yet the humdrum duties of a country clergyman did
not still his longing to know and understand the truth.
He visited the sick, closed the eyes of the dead, kept his
parish register. But his heart was in mathematics. In the
back of the old church register he recorded long rows
of figures as he worked at some astronomical problem.
In the upper floor of the barn, in back of his old, dilapi-
dated farmhouse, he cut holes in the roof to watch the
stars. They came out for him nightly and moved in
majesty across the sky. "They do me great honor," he
said. "I am forbidden to converse with great men, but
God has ordered for me a procession."

While the whole town slept, he watched the heavens
and made minute records of his observations. He
digested all that had been written on the subject of
astronomy. Slowly and patiently he tested every hypoth-

esis with his rude and improvised instruments. "Surely God will not damn me for wanting to know the truth about His glorious works," he used to say. "To look at the sky, and behold the wondrous works of God, must make a man bow his head and heart in silence. I have thought, and studied, and worked for years, and I know so little – all I can do is to adore when I behold this unfailing regularity, this miraculous balance and perfection of adaptation. The majesty of it all humbles me into the dust."

The simple, hard-working gardeners with whom he lived had a reverent awe for the great man. They guessed his worth, but still had suspicions of his sanity. They took his nightly vigils for a sort of religious ecstasy, and a wholesome fear made them quite unwilling to disturb him. So passed the days, and from a lighthearted, ambitious man, Copernicus had grown old and bowed, and nearly blind from continuously watching the stars at night.

But his work, *On the Revolutions,* was at last complete. For forty years he had worked at it, and for twenty-seven years, he himself said, not a day or night had passed without his having added something to it.

He felt that he had in this book told the truth. If men wanted to know the facts about the heavens they would find them here. He had built a science of astronomy he knew would stand secure.

But what should he do with all this mass of truth he had discovered? It was in his own brain, and it was in the hundreds and hundreds of pages of this book, which he had rewritten five times. In a few years at most his brain would be stilled in death. In five minutes, ignorance and malice might reduce the book to ashes and a lifetime of labor go for naught.

At last, at the urging of friends, he decided to send the manuscript to the city of Nuremberg to be printed. Hoping to free himself from accusations of heresy, he dedicated his work to Pope Paul III, who was a scholar and himself a lover of astronomy. "I am fully aware, Holy Father," he wrote, "that as soon as they hear that in these volumes of mine about the revolutions of the spheres of the universe I attribute some sort of motion to the Earth, some persons will immediately raise a cry of condemnation against me… It will be a simple matter for you by your authority and your judgment to suppress attacks by slanderous tongues, although – as the proverb has it – there is no cure for the bite of a false accuser."

How would the world receive the book? Copernicus could only guess and wait.

The months went by, and fear, anxiety, and suspense had their say. He was stricken with fever. In his delirium he called out, "The book – tell me – they surely have not burned it – you know I wrote no word but truth!"

On May 24, 1543, a messenger arrived from Nuremberg. He carried a copy of the printed book. He was admitted to the sick room, where he placed the volume in the hands of the stricken man. It is said that a gleam of sanity came to Copernicus. He smiled and, taking the book, gazed upon it, stroked its cover as though caressing it, opened it, and turned the leaves. Then closing the volume and holding it to his heart, he closed his eyes, and sank to sleep, to wake no more.

Did Copernicus know that his book was the door to a whole new world and that he had opened the universe to future generations? He had worked in silence and obscurity, ridiculed by those who thought he was a madman. But he was a prophet and pioneer of a new age of science, in which the glory of God in creation would be revealed in all its grandeur.

It takes courage and daring to open a new world of knowledge and to tackle difficult projects. How are you afraid of the new and different? In what way was Nicolaus Copernicus a prophet?

The writer Katherine Mansfield lived only thirty-five years, the last five of which she suffered from tuberculosis. Before her death, she described what pain and suffering had taught her.

KATHERINE MANSFIELD

I should like this to be accepted as my confession. There is no limit to human suffering. When one thinks, "Now I have touched the bottom of the sea – now I can go no deeper," one goes deeper. And so it is forever. I thought last year in Italy, any shadow more would be death. But this year has been so much more terrible that I think with affection of the Casetta! Suffering is boundless, it is eternity. One pang is eternal torment.

Physical suffering is – child's play. To have one's breast crushed by a great stone – one could laugh!

I do not want to die without leaving a record of my belief that suffering can be overcome. For I do believe it. What must one do? There is no question of what is called "passing beyond it." This is false.

One must submit. Do not resist. Take it. Be overwhelmed. Accept it fully. Make it part of life.

Everything in life that we really accept undergoes a change. So suffering must become Love. This is the mystery. This is what I must do. I must pass from personal love to greater love. I must give to the whole of life what I gave to one. The present agony will pass – if it doesn't kill. It won't last. Now I am like a man who has had his heart torn out – but – bear it – bear it! As in the physical world, so in the spiritual world, pain does not last forever. It is only so terribly acute now. It is as though a ghastly accident had happened. If I can cease reliving all the shock and horror of it, cease going over it, I will get stronger.

Here, for a strange reason, rises the figure of Doctor Sorapure. He was a good man. He helped me not only to bear pain, but he suggested that perhaps bodily ill-health is necessary, is a repairing process, and he was always telling me to consider how man plays but a part in the history of the world. My simple kindly doctor was pure of heart as Tchekhov was pure of heart. But for these ills one is one's own doctor. If "suffering" is not a repairing process, I will make it so. I will learn the lesson it teaches. These are not idle words. These are not the consolations of the sick.

Life is a mystery. The fearful pain will fade. I must turn to work. I must put my agony into something, change it. "Sorrow shall be changed into joy."

It is to lose oneself more utterly, to love more deeply, to feel oneself part of life – not separate.

O Life! accept me – make me worthy – teach me.

A prophet is very often someone who teaches us to look at things differently. In what way is Katherine Mansfield a teacher? A prophet? Read this essay again carefully. What do think she is saying? What does this story say to you?

In her suffering, Katherine Mansfield is acting as a prophet to herself. Have you ever done that? Explain.

JOHN LEARY

On August 31, 1982, John Leary was jogging home from his job at the Pax Christi Center in Cambridge to Haley House, the Catholic Worker community in Boston where he lived. It was a run he made every day. But this day he did not complete the trip. Without warning he went into cardiac arrest and died almost instantly. He was twenty-four years old. In subsequent days and at his funeral at the Melkite Cathedral in Boston, his friends were joined not only in sorrow at the brevity of his life cut short, but in wonder for all that he had accomplished and for the many lives he had touched in such a short time.

It was well known that John divided his time between peace work at the Pax Christi Center and his life of community among the poor at Haley House. But these were only a small part of his many activities on behalf of peace and justice. During the six years since he had arrived in Boston as a student at Harvard College, he had worked with prisoners, the homeless, the elderly. He had engaged in protests over the military draft, capital punishment, and abortion. He regarded all such issues to be joined in a "seamless garment" approach to the defense of human life.

Not all agreed with his every stand. But no one who met John Leary could fail to admire his idealism and his heroic determination to put his ideals into action. Just before his death he had graduated with honors from Harvard in religious studies. To his embarrassment he had received Harvard's Ames Award for service to the greater community. But even while studying at this prestigious center of learning, he had been sharing his apartment with street people and maintaining a weekly vigil at a local military research lab (for which he was twice arrested).

A mere recital of John Leary's activities gives no sense of his personality and the impact he made on others. He was kind and generous in small things as well as large. There was nothing "driven" or compulsive in his efforts. On the contrary, he seemed to reflect the saying that "angels can fly because they take themselves so lightly." Anyone meeting Leary was struck by his joyfulness, his modesty, and a wisdom that belied his youth. According to Sister Evelyn Ronan, a Catholic chaplain at Harvard, "You could look into those eyes and see all the way, right to heaven – the goodness was so powerful and the honesty unlike anyone I've ever met."

What was the meaning of this short life? According to a friend, the Reverend Peter Gomes of Harvard, "The difference with John was that he discovered that life had no purpose, no meaning, no direction, and no focus apart from the purpose and focus of God… He became in his short life the complete and total man for others, and those who knew him and loved him testify to the love of Christ that shone in and through him."

John Leary discovered his life as a prophet in the world in which he lived. He acted as a prophet, not in what he said, but in what he did. What can you learn from his life? How can you be a prophet in your world?

CHAPTER

6

Jeremiah's Message

O Lord,

So long as the weather is reasonably fine,

So long as I have no visitors,

So long as nobody asks me to do any work,

So long as I can sit in the back pew undisturbed,

So long as they don't choose hymns that I don't know,

So long as I can get home in time for play,

So long as I am not asked to do anything,

I will honor You with my presence in Church

Whenever I feel like it. Amen.

– DAVID HEAD

Most of us learn sooner or later that not everything is under our control. We have to do things we don't like, get pushed around by others, and accept things that are painful and difficult. It is hard for us to believe that these things are for our own good, that they can help us to grow, to develop strength in the face of hardships, and to face the future with courage.

Jeremiah had to deliver a harsh message to the Jewish people at a very difficult time. The king of Babylonia was marching on Jerusalem and was going to capture the city, destroy the temple, and hold the Hebrew people captive. Jeremiah then told them something that was even harder for them to accept: It was a punishment from God. He described this punishment for their infidelity in the following words:

> Like a basket full of birds,
>
> Your houses are full of treachery,
>
> So you have become great and rich,
>
> You have grown fat and lazy,
>
> There is no limit to your wickedness,
>
> You do not judge with justice,
>
> You have no concern for the orphan,
>
> You do not defend the rights of the needy...
>
>   I will refine you and test you,
>
> What else can I do for the people that I love?
>
> See what you have become!
>
> – JEREMIAH 5:27-28

Sometimes we are the architects of our own destruction, and we will listen to no one. That is what happened with the people of Israel. God had made a sacred covenant with them, and they had broken it. They were blinded by their wealth and prosperity. They had lost all feeling for the suffering of others.

They piled up riches and lived in their plush mansions. Every commandment God had graciously given them was cast aside. They had turned from God.

But God's punishment was not intended for destruction. Instead, it was strong medicine for their healing, for their return to Him and to their senses. But the healing would be long and painful. God told them through Jeremiah,

> I thought
>
> How I would set you among My sons,
>
> And give you a pleasant land,
>
> The most glorious inheritance among the nations,
>
> That you would see and call Me "My Father"
>
> And would not turn from following Me.
>
> – JEREMIAH 3:19

Jesus taught us to call God "Our Father," and that is one of the finest images we have of Him. Jeremiah says the same thing, but it goes deeper than just calling Him "Father." It also means behaving like a good child. There is an old Irish poem that says,

> Be thou my wisdom, Thou my true word,
>
> I ever with Thee, Thou with my, Lord.
>
> Thou my true Father, I Thy dear son,
>
> I with Thee dwelling, Thou with me one.

That is what Jeremiah is talking about.

THE PIG BROTHER

There was once a child who was untidy. He left his books on the floor, and his muddy shoes on the table. He put his fingers in the jam pots, and spilled ink on his best shirt. There was really no end to his untidiness.

One day the Tidy Angel came to his nursery.

"This will never do," said the Angel. "This is really shocking. You must go out and stay with your brother while I set things right here."

"I have no brother!" said the child.

"Yes, you have!" said the Angel. "You may not know him, but he will know you. Go out in the garden and watch for him, and he will soon come."

"I don't know what you mean," said the child, but he went out into the garden and waited.

Presently a squirrel came along, whisking his tail.

"Are you my brother?" asked the child.

The squirrel looked him over carefully.

"Well, I should hope not!" he said. "My fur is neat and smooth, my nest is handsomely made and in perfect order, and my young ones are properly brought up. Why do you insult me by asking such a question?"

He whisked off, and the child waited.

Presently a wren came hopping by.

"Are you my brother?" asked the child.

"No indeed!" said the wren. "What impertinence! You will find no tidier person than I in the whole garden. Not a feather is out of place, and my eggs are the wonder of all for smoothness and beauty. Brother, indeed!" He hopped off, ruffling his feathers, and the child waited.

By and by a large Tommy Cat came along.

"Are you my brother?" asked the child.

"Go and look at yourself in the glass," said the Tommy Cat haughtily, "and you will have your answer. I have been washing myself in the sun all the morning, while it is clear that no water has come near you for a long time. There are no such creatures as you in my family, I am humbly thankful to say."

He walked on, waving his tail, and the child waited.

Presently a pig came trotting along.

The child did not ask the pig if he were his brother, but the pig did not wait to be asked.

"Hallo, brother!" he grunted.

"I am not your brother!" said the child.

"Oh, yes, you are!" said the pig. "I confess I am not proud of you, but there is no mistaking the members of our family. Come along, and have a good roll in the barnyard! There is some lovely black mud there."

"I don't like to roll in mud!" said the child.

"Tell that to the hens!" said the pig brother. "Look at your hands, and your shoes, and your shirt! Come along, I say! You may have some of the pig swill for supper, if there is more than I want."

"I don't want pig swill!" said the child, and he began to cry.

Just then the Tidy Angel came out.

"I have set everything right," she said, "and it so must stay. Now, will you go with the Pig Brother, or will you come back with me, and be a tidy child?"

"With you, with you!" cried the child, and he clung to the Angel's dress.

The Pig Brother grunted.

"Small loss," he said. "There will be all the more swill for me." And he trotted on.

THE PRINCE'S HAPPY HEART

Once upon a time there was a little Prince in a country far away. He was one of the happiest little Princes who ever lived. All day long he laughed and sang and played. His voice was as sweet as music. His footsteps brought joy wherever he went. Every one thought that this was due to magic. Hung about the Prince's neck on a gold chain was a wonderful heart. It was made of gold and set with precious stones.

The godmother of the little Prince had given the heart to him when he was very small. She had said as she slipped it over his curly head, "To wear this happy heart will keep the Prince happy always. Be careful that he does not lose it."

All the people who took care of the little Prince were very careful to see that the chain of the happy heart was clasped. But one day they found the little Prince in his garden, very sad and sorrowful. His face was wrinkled into an ugly frown.

"Look!" he said, and he pointed to his neck. Then they saw what had happened.

The happy heart was gone. No one could find it, and each day the little Prince grew more sorrowful. At last they missed him. He had gone, himself, to look for the lost happy heart that he needed so much.

The little Prince searched all day. He looked in the city streets and along the country roads. He looked in the shops and in the doors of the houses where rich people lived. Nowhere could he find the heart that he had lost. At last it was almost night. He was very tired and hungry. He had never before walked so far, or felt so unhappy.

Just as the sun was setting the little Prince came to a tiny house. It was very poor and weather stained. It stood on the edge of the forest. But a bright light streamed from the windows. So he lifted the latch, as a Prince may, and went inside.

There was a mother rocking a baby to sleep. The father was reading a story out loud. The little daughter was setting the table for supper. A boy of the Prince's own age was tending the fire. The mother's dress was old. There were to be only porridge and potatoes for supper. The fire was very small. But all the family were as happy as the little Prince wanted to be. Such smiling faces and light feet the children had. How sweet the mother's voice was!

"Won't you have supper with us?" they begged. They did not seem to notice the Prince's ugly frown.

"Where are your happy hearts?" he asked them.

"We don't know what you mean," the boy and the girl said.

"Why," the Prince said, "to laugh and be as happy as you are, one has to wear a gold chain about one's neck. Where are yours?"

Oh, how the children laughed! "We don't need to wear gold hearts," they said. "We all love each other very much, and we play that this house is a castle and that we have turkey and ice cream for supper. After supper mother will tell us stories. That is all we need to make us happy."

"I will stay with you for supper," said the little Prince.

So he had supper in the tiny house that was a castle. And he played that the porridge and potatoes were turkey and ice cream. He helped to wash the dishes, and then they all sat about the fire. They played that the small fire was a great one, and listened to fairy stories that the mother told. All at once the little Prince began to smile. His laugh was just as merry as it used to be. His voice was again as sweet as music.

He had a very pleasant time, and then the boy walked part of the way home with him. When they were almost to the palace gates, the Prince said,

"It's very strange, but I feel just exactly as if I had found my happy heart."

The boy laughed. "Why, you have," he said. "Only now you are wearing it inside."

Prophets don't always predict things; they also point the way to something that happens in our lives. How do these two stories "prophesy"? What do they prophesy? What do they tell you about your own life and happiness?

7

Broken Covenants

May your Spirit guide my mind,
May its lethargy be healed,
May my mind be set to find
God in everything revealed.
Spirit, stimulate my soul,
Lift its listless muscle-tone,
With my soul in your control,
God in everything is known.
May your Spirit melt my heart,
Cold as ice and hard as steel;
Warm my heart till by your art
Christ in everything I feel.

– JOHN FRAYLINGHAUSEN

Jeremiah's message told of the disaster that would strike the people of Israel because of their infidelity to God: They had broken their covenant with Him because of their love of wealth and power, and they would not listen to the prophets sent by God to warn them. The destruction of Jerusalem and the exile of its people was the disaster needed to make them come to their senses.

Jeremiah reminded the people of God's promise and warned them of His wrath: "Listen to My voice; carry out all My orders; then you will be My people and I shall be your God...and I will fulfill the promise that I swore to your ancestors to give them a country flowing with milk and honey. (Jeremiah 11:4-5) For when I brought your ancestors out of Egypt I solemnly warned them, 'Listen to My voice,' but they would not listen, they did not pay attention, but followed their own stubborn and wicked inclinations... The house of Israel and the house of Judah have broken the covenant I made with their ancestors. I shall now bring disaster upon them." (Jeremiah 7-8, 10, 11)

The disaster, the punishment from their God, would last only a short time, long enough for His people to reflect upon their covenant with Him. The desert would bloom like a garden, and they would return to a land flowing with milk and honey. He would then make a new covenant with them – a covenant that would last forever. No offense could destroy the love of their Creator, and He would redeem them from all their iniquities.

But the punishment would come. Josiah, the king of Judah, had worked hard to unify the split kingdom of David, and Jeremiah praised him for this. But when the threat from the Assyrians came, Josiah watched as Assyria itself was threatened by the greater kingdom of Babylonia. The Pharaoh of Egypt rushed north through the land of Judah to join forces with Assyria to turn back the Babylonians. This is when Josiah made a terrible mistake. He led an army to fight the Egyptians at Megiddo. His army was roundly defeated, and Josiah was killed.

The Egyptians made a vassal of Judah and set up a puppet king, Jehoiakim. Then the political fortunes changed. The Babylonian king, Nebuchadnezzar, defeated the Egyptians and marched on Jerusalem. The king was assassinated, and the leaders of the city and most of the people were deported to Babylon. Jeremiah went into exile in Egypt, his prophecies coming true in all their horror.

One of those taken captive to Babylon was a prophet named Ezekiel. It was his voice that would be raised to give hope to the people and assure them that their God had not deserted them.

Fidelity to God – that is the chief message of these prophets. Fidelity to God is the only security, even in difficult and dangerous times. This was a hard lesson for the Jewish people to learn, as it is difficult for all of us. What are some ways in which we can be unfaithful?

CHICO MENDES

Chico Mendes, who was assassinated in 1988, was the leader of a movement linking the defense of the Amazon region with justice for the poor who lived there. Living in the state of Acre in the Amazonian region of Northwest Brazil, he organized a union of the region's rubber tappers and other poor families who earned their meager living by extracting the renewable resources of the rainforest. Mendes was himself the son of tappers who arrived in the Amazon to take advantage of the rubber boom between the two World Wars. In more recent years the fate of such workers was threatened by big landowners and ranchers who preferred to burn and clear the forests to make way for cattle.

Mendes began organizing the rubber workers in 1977. At first his aim was simply to protect their rights and livelihood. But he gradually expanded his concerns to encompass a wider ecological vision. The burning of the forest contributed to the "greenhouse effect." It ruined the land and ultimately threatened the survival of the whole planet. Thus, he made the connection between the "cry of the poor" and the "cry of the Earth."

The owners resorted to threats and brutal violence to break the will of the union. But the nonviolent tactics of Mendes and his supporters began to attract international support. Mendes himself was repeatedly threatened with death. According to his wife, Ilza, "Sometimes I'd say to Chico, 'Chico, they're going to kill you! Why don't you take care of yourself and go away?' But Chico wasn't afraid of death. He told me that he would never stop defending the Amazon forest – never!"

In 1987 Mendes was awarded the United Nations' Global 500 Award for Environmental Protection. He was called "the Gandhi of the Amazon." Soon after this the government of Brazil granted reserve status to four areas of the rainforest. But this was not enough to protect the life of Chico Mendes. On December 22, 1988, he was shot and killed by a rancher and his son.

His widow observed, "Chico had a lot of faith. When he died, I was filled with despair. But God comforted me and inspired me to work alongside others to carry on Chico's work. They killed him, but they didn't kill his ideals or crush the struggle."

How was Chico Mendes a prophet? Where does such passion for doing the right thing come from? What is God calling you to be passionate about saving or protecting? Explain.

ABRAHAM LINCOLN'S LAST DAY

The gaunt man, Abraham Lincoln, woke one morning
From a new dream that yet was an old dream
For he had known it many times before
And, usually, its coming prophesied
Important news of some sort, good or bad,
Though mostly good as he remembered it.

He had been standing on the shadowy deck
Of a black formless boat that moved away
From a dim bank, into wide, gushing waters –
River or sea, but huge – and as he stood,
The boat rushed into darkness like an arrow,
Gathering speed – and as it rushed, he woke.

He found it odd enough to tell about
That day to various people, half in jest
And half in earnest – well, it passed the time
And nearly everyone had some pet quirk,
Knocking on wood or never spilling salt,
Ladders or broken mirrors or a Friday,
And so he thought he might be left his boat,
Especially now, when he could breathe awhile
With Lee surrendered and the war stamped out
And the long work of binding up the wounds
Not yet begun – although he had his plans
For that long healing, and would work them out
In spite of all the bitter-hearted fools
Who only thought of punishing the South
Now she was beaten.

     But this boat of his.
He thought he had it.

     "Johnston has surrendered.
It must be that, I guess – for that's about
The only news we're waiting still to hear."
He smiled a little, spoke of other things.
That afternoon he drove beside his wife
And talked with her about the days to come
With curious simplicity and peace.

Well, they were getting on, and when the end
Came to his term, he would not be distressed.
They would go back to Springfield, find a house,
Live peaceably and simply, see old friends,
Take a few cases every now and then.
Old Billy Herndon's kept the practice up,
I guess he'll sort of like to have me back.
We won't be skimped, we'll have enough to spend,
Enough to do – we'll have a quiet time,
A sort of Indian summer of our age.

He looked beyond the carriage, seeing it so,
Peace at the last, and rest.

They drove back to the White House, dressed and ate,
Went to the theater in their flag-draped box.
The play was a good play, he liked the play,
Laughed at the jokes, laughed at the funny man
With the long, weeping whiskers.
      The time passed.
The shot rang out. The crazy murderer
Leaped from the box, mouthed out his Latin phrase,
Brandished his foolish pistol and was gone.

Lincoln lay stricken in the flag-draped box.
Living but speechless. Now they lifted him

And bore him off. He lay some hours so.
Then the heart failed. The breath beat in the throat.
The black, formless vessel carried him away.

– STEPHEN VINCENT BENET

Prophets are ordinary men and women who have to speak out and cry – for justice, or for peace, or for the end of suffering, or for some other noble cause. Abraham Lincoln was one of our country's greatest prophets…and he died because of it. What is this poem saying about him? What dream did he have for his old age after his term of office as president was over?

CHAPTER 8

Handling Hardships

O God, animate us to cheerfulness.

May we have a joyful sense of our own blessings,

Learn to look on the bright circumstances of our lot,

And maintain a perpetual contentedness dangers
    and hardships.

Fortify our minds against disappointment and calamity.

Preserve us from despondency, from yielding to
    dejection.

Teach us that no evil is intolerable but a guilty
    conscience,

And that nothing can hurt us,

If, with true loyalty of affection

We keep Your Commandments,

And take refuge in You. Amen.

– WILLIAM ELLERY CHANNING

After the destruction of Jerusalem and the taking of all the
Hebrews into captivity to Babylon, the prophet Jeremiah stood
over the ruined city, perhaps from the Mount of Olives, and
poured out his heart in sadness and grief. The city was
destroyed, the temple in ruins, and the people and their leaders driven into exile. Jeremiah's heart was broken at the punishment God had given to His people. He could only weep
over the greatest tragedy that had fallen on the Jewish people
in their whole history.

His words (in Lamentations 1) are bitter and sad, for the
glory that God gave to His people had been torn down, and
only a ruin remained where there had once been a great city.

> How deserted she sits,
>> the city once thronged with people!
> Once the greatest of nations,
>> she is now like a widow.
> Once the princess of nations,
>> she is now forced to hard labor.
>
> All night long she is weeping,
>> tears running down her cheeks.
> Not one of all her lovers
>> remains to comfort her.
> Her friends have all betrayed her
>> and become her enemies.
>
> Judah has gone into exile
>> after much pain and toil.

Living among the Gentiles,
　　she finds no relief.
Her persecutors all overtake her,
　　and there is no way out.

The roads to Zion are mourning;
　　no one comes to her festivals now.
Her gateways are all deserted,
　　her priests groan.
Her young girls are grief-stricken,
　　she suffers bitterly.

Her enemies now have the upper hand,
　　her enemies prosper.
For the Lord has made her suffer,
　　for the multitude of her crimes.
Her children have gone away into captivity,
　　driven in front of the oppressor.

From the daughter of Zion
　　all her splendor is gone.
Her princes were like stags
　　which could find no pasture.
Exhausted, they flee
　　before the one who hunts them down.

All her people are groaning,
　　looking for something to eat.

They have bartered their treasures for food
>> to keep them from starving.
"Look, Lord, and consider,
>> how despised I am!"

"All you who pass by on the way,
>> look and see:
Is there any sorrow like the sorrow
>> inflicted on me.
See how the Lord has struck me
>> on the day of His burning anger."

And all through the lamentations, there is the cry: "Jeru-sha-layim! Jeru-sha-layim! Shah-vu Adon-ai elo-hay-ka!"

"Jerusalem! Jerusalem! Return to the Lord your God!"

Weighted down with almost intolerable sufferings, Jeremiah sent forth a word of hope. He had this hope because he was speaking to God: the God Who saves, the God Who punishes and raises up again, the God Who loved Israel with an undying love. The people of Judah had to suffer bitterly for deserting their God, but that was not the end. The punishment was not for their destruction, but for their glorious restoration when they returned to their senses. They had, however, to endure the bitter pain of exile until they realized that their only hope was in their God.

Thus says the Lord:
I have loved you with an everlasting love,
And I shall maintain My faithful love for you.

I shall build you once more, yes, you shall be rebuilt,
O Virgin Israel!
Once more decked out in your splendid clothes,
And with your tambourines,
You will go dancing merrily.
Once more you will plant vineyards on the mountains
of Samaria.
A day will come when the watchmen shout on the
mountains of Ephraim
"Up! Let us go up to Zion to the Lord our God!"

Shout with joy for Jacob!
Hail! the chief of the nations!
Lift up your voice! Hallel! Hallel! Shout it aloud!
The Lord has saved His people, the remnant of Israel!"

– JEREMIAH 31:3-7

The clear message is that hardships are never for their own sake. They are not for our destruction. We must put our backs to the burden, knowing that the burden will be lifted by Him who gave it. Patience, patience, patience. Patience under hardship and suffering is the way to salvation, and God never deserts those who trust in and place all their hopes in Him.

It is worth reading the Lamentations of Jeremiah aloud, and entering into his feelings as he watches the destruction of his city and nation, at the same time lifting his eyes in hope to the God of Israel. They show a pattern of how we should face hardships. We should turn to God when the going gets rough.

"Cry aloud to God until He turns toward you" is the message of Jeremiah. Make fidelity to Him your armor and your shield.

HANS AND SOPHIE SCHOLL

In the summer and fall of 1942, the citizens of Munich were astonished by a series of leaflets that began to circulate throughout the city. Slipped into mailboxes by unknown hands, left in empty bus stops or on park benches, the leaflets contained a sweeping indictment of the Nazi regime and enjoined readers to work for the defeat of their own nation. At a time when the merest hint of private dissent was a treasonable offense, the audacity of this open call to resistance threw the Gestapo into a rage.

Contrary to the suspicions of the authorities, the authors of these leaflets, who called themselves simply "The White Rose," were not members of any sophisticated organization. They were in fact a few dozen university students who had been inspired by the Christian faith and the uncorrupted idealism of youth to challenge the edifice of tyranny. At the center of the group were a brother and sister, Hans and Sophie Scholl, only twenty-four and twenty-one years old. Hans was a medical student who had served on the Russian front. Sophie studied philosophy. Discerning with uncommon clarity the depth of Nazi depravity, they had decided to wage a spiritual war against the system, armed with no other weapons than courage, the power of truth, and an illegal duplicating machine. Their strategy was simple. At the very least they hoped to shatter the illusion of unanimous consent and to defy the Nazis' claim to omnipotence. Beyond that, they dared hope that by proclaiming the truth they might break the spell in which all Germany was enthralled and inspire those with doubts to move toward active resistance.

Hans and Sophie were devout Christians. They believed that the struggle against Hitler was a battle for the soul of Germany, and thus a duty for all Christians. As one of their leaflets read, "Everywhere and at all times of greatest trial men have appeared, prophets and saints who cherished their freedom, who preached the one God and who with His help brought the people to a reversal of their downward course. Man is free, to be sure, but without the true God he is defenseless against the principle of evil... We must attack evil where it is strongest, and it is "strongest in the power of Hitler... We will not be silent. We are your bad conscience. The White Rose will not leave you in peace."

Emboldened by the furor caused by their leaflets, members of the White Rose began to make other dangerous gestures, such as writing "Down with Hitler" on street signs and the walls of buildings. It was perhaps inevitable that the circle of amateurs would be discovered. The end began on February 18, 1943, when Hans and Sophie were caught distributing leaflets outside a lecture hall in the university. Under arrest and realizing that their fates were sealed, they proceeded to confess to all the actions of the White Rose, thus hoping to spare other conspirators from discovery. Despite their efforts, however, the Gestapo quickly rounded up the rest of the circle, both in Munich and in Hamburg, where an allied cell had formed.

Hans and Sophie Scholl, along with their fellow conspirator Christoph Probst, a twenty-three-year-old medical student, were quickly convicted of treason and sentenced to death. All witnesses attest to the extraordinary poise with which Hans and Sophie met their fate. Their bravery was based not on just a confidence in the verdict of history, but on a deep faith that the executioner's block was the entry to freedom and eternal life. They were beheaded on February 22.

Hans and Sophie Scholl were prophets during a time of great evil: the Nazi regime in Germany. They spoke out against the tyranny and terror in their country and the slaughter of innocent people in the name of the state. Prophets often end up being killed for their courage. The Scholls followed their consciences to their final conclusion. What do you think of their courage? Would you have done the same thing in their circumstances? Have you ever had to suffer for doing something right? Explain.

ANNE HUTCHINSON

The Puritans who settled Massachusetts in the 1630s were motivated in part by a desire to escape religious persecution. But they did not come to create a haven of religious freedom. On the contrary, they believed their holy commonwealth would stand as "a city on a hill," a beacon of purified Christianity in which biblical values of piety and sobriety would govern the conduct of its members. Severe punishment awaited those who fell short of these standards, a fate that was extended too to those who criticized the Puritan code. Rarely was there ever such a concentration of persons so godly, so sober, and so eager to cast the first stone. Among the most famous victims of Puritan justice was Anne Hutchinson, a mystic and healer, whose particular heresy was to maintain that it was a blessing and not a curse to be a woman.

Anne Hutchinson arrived in Boston in 1634, accompanied by her husband, William, a prosperous businessman, and their several children. They were committed Puritans, though of the two, Anne was by far the more zealous. She was an unusually independent woman for her times, a skilled midwife with a particular gift for herbal treatments. She was also an avid student of the Bible, which she freely interpreted in the light of what she termed divine inspiration. Though she generally adhered to the principles of Puritan orthodoxy, she held extremely advanced notions about the equality and rights of women. These positions had put her in some tension, not only with the established church of England, but also with her own co-religionists. Nevertheless, she had decided to emigrate in the belief that New England afforded greater religious freedom as well as wider opportunities for women.

In Boston the Hutchinsons quickly achieved a prominent social position. Anne's services as a midwife were in great demand, and many a family soon found themselves in her debt. Before long she also began inviting women to join her in her home for prayer and religious conversation. In time these meetings became extremely popular, attracting as many as eighty participants a week. Hutchinson would present a text from the Bible and offer her own commentary. Often her spiritual interpretation differed widely from the learned but legalistic reading offered from the Sunday pulpit. In particular, Hutchinson constantly challenged the standard interpretation of the story of Adam and Eve. This was a vital text for the Puritans, key to the doctrine of original sin. But it was regularly cited to assign special blame to women as the source of sin and to justify the extremely patriarchal structure of Puritan society.

Increasingly, the ministers opposed Hutchinson's meetings, ostensibly on the grounds that such "unauthorized" religious gatherings might confuse the faithful. But gradually the opposition was expressed in openly misogynistic terms. Hutchinson was a modern "Jezebel" who was infecting the women with perverse and "abominable" ideas regarding their dignity and rights. Anne paid no attention to her critics. When they cited the biblical texts on the need for women to keep silent in church, she rejoined with a verse from Titus permitting that "the elder women should instruct the younger."

In 1637 she was brought to trial for her subversive views. She was forty-six at the time and advanced in her fifteenth pregnancy. Nevertheless she was forced to stand for several days before a board of male interrogators as they tried desperately to get her to admit her secret blasphemies. They accused her of violating the fifth commandment – to "honor thy father and mother"

– by encouraging dissent against the fathers of the commonwealth. It was charged that by attending her gatherings, women were being tempted to neglect the care of their own families.

Anne deftly parried and defended herself until it was clear that there was no escape from the court's predetermined judgment. Cornered, she addressed the court with her own judgment:

> "You have no power over my body, neither can you do me any harm. I fear none but the great Jehovah, which hath foretold me of these things, and I do verily believe that he will deliver me out of your hands... Therefore, take heed how you proceed against me; for I know that for this you go about to do to me, God will ruin you and your posterity, and this whole state."

This outburst brought forth angry jeers. She was called a heretic and an instrument of the devil. In the words of one minister, "You have stepped out of your place, you have rather been a husband than a wife, a preacher than a hearer, and a magistrate than a subject."

Anne was held in prison during the cold winter months. Her family and a stream of sympathizers continued to visit her, and to them she continued freely to impart her spiritual teaching. In the spring she was banished from the commonwealth along with her youngest children. After seven days of difficult travel through the wilderness they arrived in Rhode Island. There they were united with William Hutchinson, who had gone ahead to establish a homestead. But soon after her arrival, Anne suffered a painful miscarriage. In Boston the details were gleefully recounted by her persecutors, who saw in her misfortune a vivid confirmation of God's judgment.

In 1642 William Hutchinson died. He had been a devoted husband throughout his wife's ordeal. When the authorities had tried to pressure him to disavow his wife's teachings, he had said "he was more nearly tied to his wife than to the church; he thought her to be a dear saint and servant of God." Alone with six of her children Anne decided to leave Rhode Island, to go as far as she could from the long arm of the Massachusetts authorities. She got as far as the Dutch settlement on Long Island. There sometime in the summer of 1643 she and her children were massacred by Indians.

Explain how Anne Hutchinson was a prophet for women's rights. How did she handle the suffering and persecution that came her way? What can you learn from her life?

JERZY POPIELUSZKO

The end of the communist era in Eastern Europe began in June 1979 when John Paul II, the newly elected Polish pope, returned to his homeland for the first of three visits. As the communist authorities stood helplessly by, millions of Poles provided the pontiff with an ecstatic welcome. His message was ostensibly spiritual, but in officially atheistic Poland the spiritual inevitably carried the weight of social criticism. There was no escaping the import of the pope's message when he proclaimed, "Do not be afraid to insist on your rights. Refuse a life based on lies and double thinking. Do not be afraid to suffer with Christ." Within a year of his visit, the militant Solidarity trade union was born.

At the time of the pope's visit Father Jerzy Popieluszko was living in Warsaw and working as a chaplain to the university medical students. Born in 1947 to a peasant family, he belonged to the generation that had grown up under communism. But while he shared with most Poles a disdain for the communist system, he had never before taken an active part in political discussions. His role in the Solidarity movement came about almost by accident. When the Gdansk ship workers went on strike in August 1980, steelworkers in Warsaw joined them in solidarity. They sent a request...for a priest to come and celebrate Mass at the factory. Father Jerzy, who happened to be on hand at the time, volunteered.

The Mass in front of the factory, where the workers had erected an enormous cross, was an extraordinary turning point in the young priest's life. At once he realized that the workers' struggle for justice and freedom was truly a spiritual struggle. It was entirely appropriate and vital that the church bear witness in the midst of this struggle. And so, with his bishop's consent, he became a chaplain to the striking workers.

In December 1981 the government declared martial law, and thousands of Solidarity members and their supporters were arrested. At this point Father Jerzy's pastoral duties expanded to include visiting the prisoners and organizing support for their families. At the same time, through his "patriotic sermons," which drew enormous crowds, he underlined the moral and spiritual dimensions of the Solidarity cause. It was a struggle for freedom and independence against foreign-imposed totalitarianism. But it was also a struggle to affirm the spiritual nature of the human person and to reject a culture based on hatred, lies, and fear.

Though the government claimed that this was no business for the church, Father Jerzy proclaimed, "It is not only the hierarchy but the millions of believers who in the broadest sense embody the church. So when people suffer and are persecuted the church also feels the pain. The mission of the church is to be with the people and to share in their joys and sorrows." As for his own vocation, he said, "To serve God is to seek a way to human hearts. To serve God is to speak about evil as a sickness which should be brought to light so that it can be cured. To serve God is to condemn evil in all its manifestations."

As his popularity grew, the government sought ways to silence him. He was subjected to countless forms of petty harassment. He was followed wherever he went. His Masses were often interrupted by provocateurs. In the most ominous attack, a bomb was hurled against his apartment. Still, he refused to be paralyzed by fear: "The only thing we should fear is the betrayal of Christ for a few silver pieces of meaningless peace."

In 1984 the pressures increased. Between January and June he was brought in for interrogation thirteen times. In July he was indicted on the charge of "abusing freedom of conscience and religion to the detriment of the Polish People's Republic." The charge provoked a storm of protest, and he was quickly offered an amnesty in honor of the fortieth anniversary of communist Poland. The workers themselves, fearful for his safety, requested that the cardinal send him abroad for study. But Father Jerzy would not consider any appearance of abandoning the workers in their time of need. He understood the risks but insisted that "if we must die it is better to meet death while defending a worthwhile cause than sitting back and letting an injustice take place... The priest is called to bear witness to the truth, to suffer for the truth, and if need be to give up his life for it. We have many such examples in Christianity. From them we should draw conclusions for ourselves."

On the night of October 19, Father Jerzy was abducted by three men who stuffed him in the trunk of their car and sped off. His driver managed to escape and report the incident. Masses were said throughout the country for the priest's safe deliverance. But it was already too late. The government, facing a propaganda debacle, launched an immediate investigation and subsequently arrested four members of the security police who led them to the priest's body. They confessed that in the early morning hours of October 20, after savagely and repeatedly beating Father Jerzy, they had tied him up, weighted his body with stones, and tossed him, still alive, into a reservoir. Those who killed Father Jerzy had wished to still his voice. But it only reverberated the louder. It was clearly heard five years later when, in the first free elections in postwar Poland, the people peacefully threw out the communist regime and elected a Solidarity government.

It should be clear by now that prophets are raised up in every age for the triumph of truth and justice and for turning people back to God. No one can tell when he or she will be called upon to be a prophet to family, friends, classmates, even acquaintances. The stories in this chapter show the courage and determination needed to speak out in the face of evil, or to turn away from evil when such a voice cries out. Choose one or two of these stories to talk about with a friend. Discuss how the main character was a prophet and what his or her message was. Compare and contrast these modern prophets with Old Testament prophets. Then name some of the ways that you could be a prophet in the world around you.

CHAPTER

Accepting Responsibility

May the lights come

To my dark heart from thy place;

May the Spirit's wisdom come

To my heart's tablet from my Savior.

Be the peace of the Spirit mine this night,

Be the peace of the Son mine this night,

Be the peace of the Father mine this night,

Each morning and evening of my life.

– A CELTIC PRAYER

The kings of Judah did not listen to either Isaiah or Jeremiah, and the disaster promised by the prophets descended on the country. Jeremiah had told them, "Babylon will be a golden cup in the Lord's hand, making all the earth drunk; the nations drank of her wine, and so they went mad." (Jeremiah 1:7)

In despair and close to death, the exiles from Judah trudged north, guarded by their captors, to a strange and unfamiliar land where the God of Judah was not known and where there was nothing but slavery and hardship. Jerusalem, the Holy City, was in ruins, the temple destroyed, and it seemed their God had deserted them.

But that was not to be. Jeremiah had prophesied that the exiles would return someday, that the city and temple would be rebuilt, but his voice was no longer among them. Instead, God raised up another prophet, Ezekiel, to be their voice of hope.

The exiles struggled with the dark problem of their destiny, recalling again and again the treasured words of the prophets and their sacred writings. Their catastrophe was not the result of Divine indifference, but of Divine justice. A change in the behavior of God's people would bring about a reversal of their misfortune.

Ezekiel was a priest who was sent into exile with the rest of the Judeans. God spoke to him, directing him to be a prophet to His rebellious people. Ezekiel became the voice of conscience for the Jewish people in exile.

Ezekiel spoke in powerful symbols and imagery to command the attention of these downcast people. He reminded them of their past infidelities and of a promised return to Jerusalem. He even told them what the rebuilt city and temple would look like. It is in Ezekiel's prophecies that there is a first mention of a Messiah-King, who would come from the house of David: "I will set over them one shepherd, my servant David, and he shall feed them. He shall feed them and be their shepherd." (Ezekiel 37:24-25)

There must be repentance, reconciliation, and a return to the keeping of God's commands. Then there will be restoration. These three themes – repentance, reconciliation, and restoration – are the themes of Ezekiel's fiery and vivid writings. In one of Ezekiel's prophecies, God showed the prophet a field covered with dried bones that symbolized the Jewish people in exile. As Ezekiel watched, the dried bones came alive and were covered with flesh, the bodies of the dead made whole and living.

Ezekiel emphasized the individual responsibility of each exile. Only by individual responsibility would the nation be restored. And Ezekiel's lesson is the same for us: We are individually responsible for the evil that we do. We must individually turn away from evil and do good. The Jewish people had to learn this truth through a hard and painful lesson. What kind of lesson does this indicate to you? What does individual responsibility mean? How does this apply to you?

Read the following account of how one man found the courage to accept the life-or-death responsibility of ferrying slaves to freedom.

ARNOLD GRAGSON

It was 'cause he used to let me go around in the day and night so much that I came to be the one who carried the runnin'-away slaves over the river. It was funny the way I started it, too.

I didn't have no idea of ever gettin' mixed up in any sort of business like that, until one special night. I hadn't even thought of rowing across the river myself.

But one night I had gone on another plantation courtin', and the old woman whose house I went to told me she had a real pretty girl there who wanted to go across the river, and would I take her? I was scared and backed out in a hurry. But then I saw the girl, and she was such a pretty little thing – brown-skinned and kinda rosy, and looking as scared as I was feelin' – so it wasn't long before I was listenin' to the old woman tell me when to take her and where to leave her on the other side.

I didn't have nerve enough to do it that night, though, and I told them to wait for me until tomorrow night. All the next day I kept seeing Mr. Tabb laying a rawhide across my back or shooting me, and kept seeing that scared little brown girl back at the house, looking at me with her big eyes and asking me if I wouldn't just row her across to Ripley, Ohio. Me and Mr. Tabb lost, and soon as dusk settled that night, I was at the old lady's house.

I don't know how I ever rowed that boat across the river. The current was strong and I was trembling. I couldn't see a thing there in the dark, but I felt that girl's eyes. We didn't dare to whisper, so I couldn't tell her how sure I was that Mr. Tabb or some of the other owners would "tear me up" when they found out what I had done. I just knew they would find out.

I was worried, too, about where to put her out of the boat. I couldn't ride her across the river all night, and I didn't know a thing about the other side. I had heard a lot about it from other slaves, but I thought it was just about like Mason County, with slaves and masters, over-seers and rawhides; and so, I just knew that if I pulled the boat up and went to asking people where to take her I would get a beating or get killed.

I don't know whether it seemed like a long time or a short time, now – it's so long ago. I know it was a long time rowing there in the cold and worryin', but it was short, too, 'cause as soon as I did get on the other side the big-eyed brown skinned girl would be gone. Well, pretty soon I saw a tall light and I remembered what the old lady had told me about looking for that light and rowing to it. I did, and when I got up to it, two men reached down and grabbed her. I started tremblin' all over again, and prayin'. Then, one of the men took my arm and I just felt down inside of me that the Lord had got ready for me. "You hungry, boy?" is what he asked me, and if he hadn't been holdin' me I think I would have fell backward into the river.

That was my first trip. It took me a long time to get over my scared feelin', but I finally did, and I soon found myself goin' back across the river with two or three people, and sometimes a whole boatload. I got so I used to make three or four trips a month.

Sometimes being a prophet takes courage, even the risk of our lives, and sometimes it is more by doing than speaking. The Underground Railroad was an act of prophecy against the evil of slavery. How have you acted in a prophetic way like the young

man in this story? What are other ways that you could be a prophet?

ELIZABETH FRY

Elizabeth Fry was raised in a prosperous Quaker family, the Gurneys of Norwich, England. Her family represented the more "lax" end of the Quaker spectrum; thus, the children were allowed to sing and dance and wear bright clothes to Meeting. As Elizabeth grew up, however, she was increasingly attracted to the more austere devotional habits of the "Plain Quakers." When she was seventeen an encounter with a Quaker abolitionist from the United States stimulated her desire to pursue a path of godly service. Afterward she wrote in her journal, "I wish the state of enthusiasm I am now in may last, for today I *have felt* there is a *God. I have been devotional,* and my mind has been led away from the follies that it is mostly wrapt up in."

Within two years she was married to Joseph Fry, and her life was subsequently absorbed in the responsibilities of a growing family. Ultimately, she bore eleven children over a period of twenty-one years. This life was not without its rewards. But after twelve years of marriage, she felt that she was missing out on her true vocation. In her diary she wrote, "I fear that my life is slipping away to little purpose."

It was soon afterward that she accepted the invitation of another Quaker to visit the infamous Newgate prison. There she witnessed conditions which filled her with shame and indignation. Women and their young children were crowded into fetid cells, "tried and untried, misdemeanants and felons" together, "in rags and dirt...sleeping without bedding on the floor." In one cell she saw two women strip the clothing off a dead baby to dress another infant.

This was the beginning of a cause public and private that Fry pursued for the rest of her life. She began by returning to the prison with clean clothing and straw for the women to lie on. Although the jailers tried to obstruct her efforts, claiming that the women were incorrigible savages, Fry was determined to respond to them in a manner befitting their humanity. When she asked them whether they would like her to provide instruction to their children, they responded eagerly, with many of the illiterate women pressing in to benefit from her lessons.

With the support of a committee of other Quaker women, Fry launched a campaign for general prison reform. This achieved many results, including provisions for larger living quarters, better food, fresh air, and the supply of sewing materials to provide the women with some occupation and a means of earning money. Over the years Fry was tireless in her efforts, which eventually extended throughout England and Scotland. There were some who criticized her on the grounds that her devotion to this cause entailed the neglect of her family. She too upbraided herself at times. As she wrote in her journal in 1817,

"My mind too much tossed by a variety of interests and duties – husband, children, household,
accounts, Meetings, the church, near relations,
friends, and Newgate – most of these things press
a good deal upon me. I hope I am not undertaking
too much, but it is a little like being in the whirlwind and in the storm."

Her efforts also elicited public opposition from
those who felt that to humanize the prisons was to
undermine their deterrent value, thus "removing the
dread of punishment in the criminal classes." But Fry
was motivated by the conviction that prisoners, regard-
less of their crimes, were human beings who bore within them the spark of the divine image. It was sacrilege
to treat them with no more than punitive cruelty. Fry
continued to live in the whirlwind and pressed on with
her cause, in season and out, until the end of her life on
October 12, 1845.

*Describe how Elizabeth Fry was a prophet. What groups in
our time are treated as less than human? How could you be a
prophetic voice for them?*

CHAPTER 10

Consequences of Infidelity to God

Be strong. Be strong.
We are not here to dream,
To drift,
There are battles to fight,
And loads to lift;
Shun not the battle,
'Tis God's gift
Be strong, be strong.
It matters not how
Deep entrenched the wrong,
How hard the fight, the day how long,
Faint not, fight on,
Tomorrow comes the song.
Be strong, be strong.

– AUTHOR UNKNOWN

Infidelity to God comes with a great price, and that was the warning that Ezekiel gave to the people of Judah during their exile in Babylonia. It was not the king of Babylonia who was responsible for their pain and punishment. It was the Lord God of heaven and earth, the God of Abraham, Isaac, and Jacob. While their punishment and exile were only temporary, they had to live godly lives amongst the heathens and turn away from their infidelities and pagan practices. They had listened to the wrong voices under their kings and ignored the warnings of their prophets. Now Ezekiel would bring the full force of God's judgment on the infidelity of His people.

And in their pain and oppression, the people listened. Armed with their sacred writings and the powerful words of their prophets, the Jewish people in exile came to terms with their fate by remaining true to their faith and nourishing hope. The Lord was with them even in exile. They separated themselves from the pagan practices of their captors, followed their own customs and traditions, and observed the Sabbath and all the ordinances of their law. Since they had no temple, they created something new: the synagogue, where they would meet for prayer and mutual encouragement. They pored over their sacred books and the words of their prophets, recalling again their history and the care of God over them. In that history, they found new themes to ponder, images to encourage them, and the living memory of Jerusalem and Judah. It was here that the rabbi, the inspired teacher who would break the bread of the word to them, replaced the priest.

"If I forget you, O Jerusalem, let my right hand wither, let my tongue cleave to the roof of my mouth, if I do not remember you, if I do not set Jerusalem above my highest joy." (from Psalm 137)

In the city of Babylon the exiles remembered their fall from and return to God, and this remembrance would remain with them long after their return to Jerusalem.

God had taken away their city, their nation, and all that He had given them because they had been unfaithful to His covenant. If they were to return, they must never again turn to their evil ways. They would have the words of the prophets to remind them of their exile. It was at this time perhaps, that the words of the prophets Isaiah, Jeremiah, and Ezekiel were written down and became part of the sacred books of the Jews. This is where the Bible was assembled into the three great divisions of the Hebrew Bible: the *Torah* (the Books of Moses), the *Prophets,* and the *Writings* (all other books). This is also where the great tradition was born of training scribes to preserve and pass on the sacred writings.

Remembering is part of all genuine religion – remembering the great works of God for the human race as a whole and for ourselves in particular. Whether we know it or not, God is hovering over us every moment of our lives. Reading the sacred books of the Bible reminds us of God's actions in history. It gives us reasons for being faithful to Him and for expecting His action in our own lives.

THE MAN WITHOUT A COUNTRY

(Here is the most despised name in American history. Benedict Arnold (1741-1801) was a descendant of a distinguished New England family and an American hero in the early part of the Revolutionary War. But he grew to love luxury, and he lusted after glory. In 1779, he began selling military information to the British, and in the summer of 1780, while in command of West Point in New York, Arnold secretly offered to surrender the fort and its garrison to the British for £20,000. The American forces discovered the plot, but Arnold managed to escape. For the rest of the war he served as a British brigadier, further blackening his name by conducting destructive raids in Virginia and his own native Connecticut. After the war, Arnold and his family sailed to England, where he gradually discovered that the disgrace of a traitor knows no national boundaries.)

Benedict Arnold sailed from his native land and returned no more. From that time forth, wherever he went, three whispered words followed him, singing through his ears into his heart – *Arnold the Traitor.*

When he stood beside the King in the House of Lords, a whisper crept through the thronged house, and as the whisper deepened into a murmur, one venerable lord arose and said he loved his sovereign, but could not speak to him while by his side stood – *Arnold the Traitor.*

He went to the theater, parading his warrior form amid the fairest flowers of British nobility and beauty; but no sooner was his face seen than the whole audience rose – the lord in his cushioned seat, the vagrant in the gallery. They rose together, while from the pit to the dome echoed the cry – *"Arnold the Traitor."*

When he issued from his gorgeous mansion, the liveried servant who ate his bread whispered in contempt to his fellow lackey, as he took his position in his master's carriage – *"Arnold the Traitor."*

Grossly insulted in a public place, he appealed to the company, and scowling at his antagonist with his fierce brow, he spat full in his face. His antagonist was a man of courage, and he said, "Time may scorn me, but I never can stain my sword by killing – *Arnold the Traitor."*

He left London. He engaged in commerce. His ships were on the ocean, his warehouses in Nova Scotia, his plantations in the West Indies. One night his warehouses were burned to ashes. The entire population of St. John's – accusing the owner of burning his own property, to defraud the insurance companies – assembled in that British town, and in sight of his very window they hanged an effigy, which bore a huge placard, inscribed – *"Arnold the Traitor."*

There was a day when Talleyrand arrived in Le Havre, hotfoot from Paris. It was in the darkest hour of the French Revolution. All who belonged to the ranks of the aristocracy were fleeing. Pursued by the bloodhounds of the Reign of Terror, stripped of his property and power, Talleyrand secured a passage to America in a ship about to sail. He was going, a beggar and a wanderer, to a strange land to earn his bread by daily labor. "Is there any American gentleman staying at your house?" he asked the landlord of his hotel. "I am about to cross the water, and would like a letter to some person of influence in the New World."

The landlord hesitated, and then said, "There is a gentleman upstairs, from either America or Britain, but whether American or Englishman I cannot tell."

He pointed the way, and Talleyrand, who during his life was bishop, prince, prime minister, ascended the stairs, knocked at the stranger's door, and entered.

In the far corner of a dimly lighted room sat a gentleman of some fifty years, his arms folded and his head bowed on his breast. From a window directly opposite, a flood of light poured over his forehead. His eyes, looking from beneath the downcast brows, gazed in Talleyrand's face with a peculiar and searching expression. His face was striking in its outline; his mouth and chin indicative of an iron will. His form was clad in a dark but rich and distinguished costume. Talleyrand advanced, stated that he was a fugitive, and, under the impression that the gentleman who sat before him was an American, he solicited his kind offices.

"I am a wanderer – an exile. I am forced to fly to the New World, without a friend or a hope. You are an American? Give me, then, I beseech you, a letter of introduction to some friend of yours, so that I may earn my bread. A gentleman like you has doubtless many friends."

The strange gentleman rose. With a look that Talleyrand never forgot, he retreated toward the door of the next chamber, saying, *"I am the only man born in the*

New World that can raise his hand and say I have not one friend – not one – in all America!"

"Who are you?" cried the exile, as the stranger retreated. "Your name?"

"My name is *Benedict Arnold.*"

He was gone. Talleyrand sank into a chair, gasping the words – *"Arnold the Traitor!"*

Thus he wandered over the earth, another Cain, with the murderer's mark upon his brow. We cannot doubt that he died friendless, and that the memory of his treachery to his native land gnawed like a cancer at his heart, murmuring, "True to your country, what might you have been, *O Arnold the Traitor!"*

What consequences did Arnold face because of his betrayal? According to Ezekiel, what consequences will we face if we are unfaithful to God?

TARPEIA

There was once a girl named Tarpeia, whose father was guard of the outer gate of the citadel of Rome. It was a time of war – the Sabines were besieging the city. Their camp was close outside the city wall.

Tarpeia used to see the Sabine soldiers when she went to draw water from the public well, for that was outside the gate. And sometimes she stayed about and let the strange men talk with her, because she liked to look at their bright silver ornaments. The Sabine soldiers wore heavy silver rings and bracelets on their left arms – some wore as many as four or five.

The soldiers knew she was the daughter of the keeper of the citadel, and they saw that she had greedy eyes for their ornaments. So day by day they talked with her, and showed her their silver rings, and tempted her. And at last Tarpeia made a bargain, to betray her city to them. She said she would unlock the great gate and let them in, *if they would give her what they wore on their left arms.*

The night came. When it was perfectly dark and still, Tarpeia stole from her bed, took the great key from its place, and silently unlocked the gate which protected the city. Outside, in the dark, stood the soldiers of the enemy, waiting. As she opened the gate, the long shadowy files pressed forward silently, and the Sabines entered the citadel.

As the first man came inside, Tarpeia stretched forth her hand for her price. The soldier lifted high his left arm. "Take thy reward!" he said, and as he spoke he hurled upon her that which he wore upon it. Down upon her head crashed – not the silver rings of the soldier, but the great brass shield he carried in battle!

She sank beneath it to the ground.

"Take thy reward," said the next, and his shield rang against the first.

"Thy reward," said the next – and the next – and the next – and the next; every man wore his shield on his left arm.

So Tarpeia lay buried beneath the reward she had claimed, and the Sabines marched past her dead body, into the city she had betrayed.

In this ancient Roman legend of treason, what consequences did Tarpeia face because of her betrayal and infidelity? What consequences will we face if we betray or are unfaithful to God?

A Message of Hope to Those in Exile

Give me good digestion, Lord,

And also something to digest.

Give me a healthy body, Lord,

With sense to keep it at its best.

Give me a healthy mind, Good Lord,

To keep the pure and good in sight,

Which, seeing sin, is not appalled,

But finds a way to set it right.

Give me a mind that is not bored,

That does not whimper, whine, or sigh,

Don't let me worry over much

About the fussy thing called "I."

Give me a sense of humor, Lord,

Give me the grace to see a joke,

To get some happiness in life,

And pass it on to other folk.

– SIR THOMAS MORE

The Jewish exiles were not just the victims of political and military might: This is what the prophets had stated again and again. But the very prophets who had predicted such disasters as the conquest of Jerusalem and the exile of the Jewish people also prophesied not only the final downfall of the great kingdom that had conquered them, but also a triumphant and victorious return to their land.

From this, the Jewish people began to take heart. They were even more encouraged as Ezekiel, who had experienced both the conquest of their country and the bitter journey into exile, began to lay a blueprint of the city and temple they would return to. "Thus says the Lord God, You, O mountains of Israel, shall shoot forth your branches and yield your fruit to My people Israel; for they will soon come home…and you shall be tilled and sown; and I will multiply men upon you, the whole house of Israel, all of it; the cities shall be inhabited and ruined places rebuilt; and I will multiply upon you man and beast, and they shall increase and be fruitful." (Ezekiel 36:8-11)

Ezekiel spoke of the restoration of Jerusalem as the center of the nation. He prophesied a rebuilt temple, as carefully drawn as an architect's blueprint, complete with every measurement of each room, door, window, wall, and gate. His words gave shape to the hopes of the exiles and their children.

These prophecies would come true more quickly than the exiles imagined. Less than fifty years after the great

Babylonian empire had conquered Judah and sent its inhabitants into exile, it suddenly collapsed after being conquered by the Persian king, Cyrus. The exiles would return and receive religious freedom, choosing their own leaders from among themselves. The city of Jerusalem would be restored and the temple rebuilt, paid for by the royal treasury. Everything Ezekiel had prophesied came true. The words of Cyrus were the royal command that made all of this possible: "Thus says Cyrus, King of Persia: Whoever among you wishes to do so, let him go up to Jerusalem, which is in Judah, and rebuild the House of the Lord, the God of Israel."

The prophets were the conscience of the Jewish people, reminding them of God's commandments and their obligations to Him. We, too, have a conscience that warns us when we do wrong, and warns us even more loudly when we continue to do wrong.

Do you listen to your conscience, or do you often ignore it? Why? It is said that the voice of conscience is the voice of God. Do you believe this? Why or why not?

The Fool's Prayer

The royal feast was done; the King
Sought some new sport to banish care,
And to his jester cried: "Sir Fool,
Kneel now, and make for us a prayer!"

The jester doffed his cap and bells,
And stood the mocking court before;

111

They could not see the bitter smile
Behind the painted grin he wore.

He bowed his head, and bent his knee
Upon the monarch's silken stool;
His pleading voice arose: "O Lord,
Be merciful to me, a fool!

"No pity, Lord, could change the heart
From red with wrong to white as wool;
The rod must heal the sin: but, Lord,
Be merciful to me, a fool!

"'Tis not by guilt the onward sweep
Of truth and right, O Lord, we stay;
'Tis by our follies that so long
We hold the earth from heaven away.

"These clumsy feet, still in the mire,
Go crushing blossoms without end;
These hard, well-meaning hands we thrust
Among the heart-strings of a friend.

"The ill-timed truth we might have kept –
Who knows how sharp it pierced and stung?
The word we had not sense to say –
Who knows how grandly it had rung?

"Our faults no tenderness should ask,
The chastening stripes must cleanse them all;
But for our blunders – oh, in shame
Before the eyes of heaven we fall.

"Earth bears no balsam for mistakes;
Men crown the knave, and scourge the tool
That did his will; but Thou, O Lord,
Be merciful to me, a fool!"

The room was hushed; in silence rose
The King, and sought his gardens cool,
And walked apart, and murmured low,
"Be merciful to me, a fool!"

– EDWARD ROWLAND SILL

In what way was the jester in this poem a prophet? What was he saying that made the king say also, "Be merciful to me, a fool"?

Do you know why kings had jesters? What could the jester say that nobody else dared to say?

Recessional

God of our fathers, known of old,
Lord of the far-flung battle-line,
Beneath whose awful hand we hold
Dominion over palm and pine –

Lord God of Hosts, be with us yet,
Lest we forget – lest we forget!

The tumult and the shouting dies;
The captains and the kings depart:
Still stands Thine ancient sacrifice,
An humble and a contrite heart.
Lord God of Hosts, be with us yet,
Lest we forget – lest we forget!

Far-called, our navies melt away;
On dune and headland sinks the fire:
Lo, all our pomp of yesterday
Is one with Nineveh and Tyre!
Judge of the Nations, spare us yet.
Lest we forget – lest we forget!

If, drunk with sight of power, we loose
Wild tongues that have not Thee in awe,
Such boastings as the Gentiles use,
Or lesser breeds without the Law –
Lord God of Hosts, be with us yet,
Lest we forget – lest we forget!

For heathen heart that puts her trust
In reeking tube and iron shard,
All valiant dust that builds on dust,
And, guarding, calls not Thee to guard,

114

For frantic boast and foolish word –

– RUDYARD KIPLING

The English poet, Kipling, wrote this poem at the height of the Victorian era in England. In what way was he a prophet? What was he reminding the people and the rulers of England about? What is he saying to you?

For My Brother Reported Missing in Action

Sweet brother, if I do not sleep

My eyes are flowers for your tomb;

And if I cannot eat my bread,

My fasts shall live like willows where you died.

If in the heat I find no water for my thirst,

My thirst shall turn to springs for you, poor traveler.

Where, in what desolate and smoky country,

Lies your poor body lost and dead?

And in what landscape of disaster

Had your unhappy spirit lost its road?

Come, in my labor find a resting place

And in my sorrows lay your head,

Or rather take my life and blood

And buy yourself a better bed

Or take my breath and take my death

And buy yourself a better rest.

When all the men of war are shot
And flags have fallen into dust,
Your cross and mine shall tell men still
Christ died on each, for both of us.

For in the wreckage of your April Christ lies slain,
And Christ weeps in the ruins of my spring:
The money of whose tears shall fall
Into your weak and friendless hand,
And buy you back to your own land:
The silence of Whose tears shall fall
Like bells upon your alien tomb.
Hear them and come: They call you home.

– SIR THOMAS MERTON

Sometimes we can be a prophet to ourselves, especially when our world seems to be falling apart. Thomas Merton wrote this poem about his dead brother. In what way is his poem like the prophecies of Ezekiel? What is he telling himself? Have you ever been a prophet to yourself? What did it help you to do?

Called Back to Fidelity

Give us grace and strength
to forbear and to persevere.
Give us courage and gaiety
and the quiet mind.
Spare to us friends, soften
to us our enemies. Bless us
if it may be in all our
innocent endeavors. If it
may not, give us the strength
to encounter that which is to
come, that we may be brave
in peril, constant in tribulation,
temperate in wrath.
And in changes of fortune
And down to the gates of death
Loyal and loving
To one another.

– ROBERT LOUIS STEVENSON

As the great Assyrian empire began to flex its political muscles seven hundred years before Christ, it began to swallow up
the smaller nations around it. One of the first to be threatened
was the northern kingdom of Israel. The great kingdom of
David and Solomon had been divided when Solomon's son,
Rehoboam, became a tyrannical king, levying heavy taxes on
his people and oppressing them with forced labor for the
extension of his kingdom. The people of the north revolted,
set up their own king, and seceded from Reheboam's tyranny.

This northern kingdom was strategically stronger than
Judah, to the south. It had access to the sea; it had a larger
population; its army was more powerful, and it had rich and
abundant resources. But its political history was a disaster.

In its short history of two hundred years, the northern
kingdom had nineteen kings, seven of whom were assassinated. It was also in constant threat from its northern neighbor,
Assyria, and was finally invaded and conquered by this powerful empire.

Hosea spoke out in the northern kingdom when the prosperity of the country brought about a passion for riches, open
immorality, the worship of their neighbor's gods, and an abandonment of the covenant with God. The Law of Moses was set
aside and forgotten, and the people began to imitate the ways
and customs of the world around them. God was completely
forgotten.

Hosea's prophetic mission began at the same time as
Isaiah's mission to Judah. He began with a shocking analogy
of how God looked upon His people: They had behaved like an
unfaithful spouse, and God was calling them back to fidelity.

They were also strongly tempted to set up political alliances with their heathen neighbors for their own protection, but Hosea told them that God was their protector and that they should seek their security in Him. These alliances would only lead them into idolatry.

Hosea told them in strong and powerful images that their only secure alliance was with God, who brought them out of the land of Egypt, gave them security, and chose a king to rule over them. Their own kings were false kings, not chosen by God, and their rule could only end in disaster for the whole nation.

Like Isaiah and Jeremiah, Hosea prophesied conquest and exile, not as a natural political consequence, but as a punishment from God for their infidelity. But there was a promise of redemption as well: "I shall cure them of their disloyalty; I shall love them with all my heart, for my anger will turn away from them... They will come back to live in my shade."

The powerful message is this: Though we may be unfaithful to God, He remains faithful to us and draws us back to Him by the bonds of a love which never fails, however deep and long our infidelity. If conscience is the voice of God, it is more than a voice of condemnation; it is voice of hope and love and tireless kindness. How often have you experienced that?

The Reverend Dr. Martin Luther King delivered the following eulogy at the funeral of three of the four young girls (Addie Mae Collins, Denise McNair, Carole Robertson, and Cynthia Wesley) who were killed on September 15, 1963, by a bomb that exploded in the basement of the 16th Street Baptist Church in Birmingham, Alabama.

THE MARTYRED CHILDREN OF BIRMINGHAM

This afternoon we gather in the quiet of this sanctuary to pay our last tribute of respect to these beautiful children of God. They entered the stage of history just a few years ago, and in the brief years that they were privileged to act on this mortal stage, they played their parts exceedingly well. Now the curtain falls; they move through the exit; the drama of their earthly life comes to a close. They are now committed back to that eternity from which they came.

These children – unoffending; innocent and beautiful – were the victims of one of the most vicious, heinous crimes ever perpetrated against humanity.

Yet they died nobly. They are the martyred heroines of a holy crusade for freedom and human dignity. So they have something to say to us in their death. They have something to say to every minister of the gospel who has remained silent behind the safe security of stained-glass windows. They have something to say to every politician who has fed his constituents the stale bread of hatred and the spoiled meat of racism. They have something to say to a federal government that has compromised with the undemocratic practices of southern Dixiecrats and the blatant hypocrisy of right-wing northern Republicans. They have something to say to every Negro who passively accepts the evil system of segregation and stands on the sidelines in the midst of a mighty struggle for justice. They say to each of us, black and white alike, that we must substitute courage for caution. They say to us that we must be concerned not merely about who murdered them, but about the system, the way of life and the philosophy which produced the murderers. Their death says to us that we must work passionately and unrelentingly to make the American dream a reality.

So they did not die in vain. God still has a way of wringing good out of evil. History has proven over and over again that unmerited suffering is redemptive. The innocent blood of these little girls may well serve as the redemptive force that will bring new light to this dark city. The holy Scripture says, "A little child shall lead them." The death of these little children may lead our whole Southland from the low road of man's inhumanity to man to the high road of peace and brotherhood. These tragic deaths may lead our nation to substitute an aristocracy of character for an aristocracy of color. The spilt blood of these innocent girls may cause the whole citizenry of Birmingham to transform the negative extremes of a dark past into the positive extremes of a bright future. Indeed, this tragic event may cause the white South to come to terms with its conscience.

So in spite of the darkness of this hour we must not despair. We must not become bitter; nor must we harbor the desire to retaliate with violence. We must not lose faith in our white brothers. Somehow we must believe that the most misguided among them can learn to respect the dignity and worth of all human personality.

May I now say a word to you, the members of the bereaved families. It is almost impossible to say anything that can console you at this difficult hour and remove the deep clouds of disappointment which are floating in your mental skies. But I hope you can find a little consolation from the universality of this experience. Death comes to every individual. There is an amazing democracy about death. It is not aristocracy for some of the people, but a democracy for all of the people. Kings die and beggars die; rich men die and poor men die; old people die and young people die; death comes to the innocent and it comes to the guilty. Death is the irreducible common denominator of all men.

I hope you can find some consolation from Christianity's affirmation that death is not the end. Death is not a period that ends the great sentence of life, but the comma that punctuates it to a more lofty significance. Death is not a blind alley that leads the human race into a state of nothingness, but an open door which leads man into life eternal. Let this daring faith, this great invincible surmise, be your sustaining power during these trying days.

At times, life is hard, as hard as crucible steel. It has its bleak and painful moments. Like the ever-flowing waters of a river, life has its moments of drought and its moments of flood. Like the ever-changing cycle of the seasons, life has the soothing warmth of the summers and the piercing chill of its winters. But through it all,

God walks with us. Never forget that God is able to lift you from fatigue of despair to the buoyancy of hope, and transform dark and desolate valleys into sunlit paths of inner peace.

Your children did not live long, but they lived well. The quantity of their lives was disturbingly small, but the quality of their lives was magnificently big. Where they died and what they were doing when death came will remain a marvelous tribute to each of you and an eternal epitaph to each of them. They died not in a den or dive nor were they hearing and telling filthy jokes at the time of their death. They died within the sacred walls of the church after discussing a principle as eternal as love.

Shakespeare had Horatio utter some beautiful words over the dead body of Hamlet. I paraphrase these words today as I stand over the last remains of these lovely girls.

"Good night, sweet princesses; may the flight of angels take thee to the eternal rest."

Martin Luther King was one of the prophets of our time. How do his words resemble those of Hosea, and what truths of God is he trying to make clear by his words? What do his words tell you about racism and hatred of others? In what way were the little girls who died saying something prophetic by their deaths?

What did Dr. King mean by the "democracy of death"? In what way is life sometimes "hard as crucible steel"? Why is the quality of someone's life more important than its quantity?

In what way was Dr. Martin Luther King the conscience of the civil rights movement?

CHAPTER

God's Compassion

Lord, lift me up,

Put me in the palm of Your hand

And unlock the chamber of my heart.

Let love come in.

Lord, I have been walking,

Lord, hold my hand, I'm tired of stumbling in

      dark alleys.

Put me in the palm of Your hand.

Lord, lift me up.

Show me that love is still around.

Lord, lift me up.

Show me that love is still around…

– JAMES MATTHEWS

The words that God spoke through Hosea are the words of a rejected lover. The words are not of bitterness, but of concern for Israel, who had rejected God. As Israel hardened its heart, God's compassion grew. The nation was in turmoil, with political factions jockeying for power, pro-Egyptian or pro-Assyrian, each seeking to gain power or to get protection from foreign powers.

> Ephraim is like a dove
> Silly and without sense,
> Calling to Egypt, going to Assyria...
> They make a bargain with Assyria,
> And oil is transported to Egypt.
>
> – HOSEA 7:11, 12:1

Their hope and solidarity was only in God, and the image that God used for the love of His people is that of marriage. This is one of the noblest ideas in the Bible. Israel was the consort of God. Here the prophet was struck with astonishment and wonder at this close relationship of God with His people, a relationship that no sin could destroy, no offense weaken.

The word that God used to describe God's love of Israel is the Hebrew word *hessed*. It is a word difficult to translate: It is more than kindness, more than compassion, more than mercy, and more than devotion. It is tenderness and love that wishes the best for the one that is loved, knowing that the loved one is intent on his or her own destruction.

> They sow the wind,
> And will reap the whirlwind.
>
> – HOSEA 8:7

126

It was I who taught you to walk,

I took you in my arms;

But they did not know that I healed them.

I led them with the cords of compassion,

With the bands of love;

With them I was like someone

Lifting an infant to his cheeks,

I bent down to them and fed them gently.

– HOSEA 11:3-4

There is something powerful and beautiful about this image: God, using His power not to punish and destroy, but to lift up and gently teach His true nature and tender concern for their welfare – the lavish generosity toward His creatures and the utter humility with which He comes before them.

Hosea, one of the first prophets, began to reveal something of the *pathos* of God, the concern He has for His creatures and the lengths He will go to call them back to Him.

The complaint of the prophet was that Israel did not know God. He coined the Hebrew expression, *daath elohim:* not just to know God, but to enter into an emotional relationship with Him by a strong attachment. The love of God requires full commitment to Him.

Is this a new idea for you? What is your concept of God's relationship with you? Did you ever think that He had a tender concern for your welfare because He loves you and you are important to Him? That is what Hosea was saying, and his words were meant not only for the ancient Israelites, but for each one of us as well.

ANNE SULLIVAN MACY

Anne Sullivan Macy's life was never easy. Born to poor Irish parents in Massachusetts in 1866, Annie had serious lifelong vision problems that were only partly helped by surgery. Her mother died when Annie was only eight, so she and her younger brother, Jimmie, were placed in the state infirmary at Tewksbury, Massachusetts. Not long after their arrival, Jimmie died in the squalid conditions. He was the only loved one left in her life, and she suffered terribly from grief and loneliness.

It was at Tewksbury that Annie first heard of special schools for the blind. After begging state officials to send her to one of them, by the age of fourteen, she was eventually sent to the Perkins Institution.

A talented and compassionate doctor named Samuel Gridley Howe was the founder of the Perkins Institution and the first to attempt educating a deaf and blind child. His pupil, Laura Bridgman was still at Perkins when Annie arrived, and because neither had any other home to go to during vacations, they spent a great deal of time together. With the help of Laura, Annie became proficient in the use of the hand alphabet.

After completing her studies, she underwent eye surgery that left her with limited vision. At the age of twenty, Annie Sullivan was both visually impaired and unemployed. Then a letter arrived from Alabama that would change Annie's existence. The letter detailed the life of a seven-year-old blind, deaf, and mute girl named

Helen Keller. Helen's parents were hopeful that a governess could be hired to help her.

Annie did not want the job, but she had no other prospects or means of supporting herself. While considering the offer, she spent a month reading the diary Dr. Howe had kept while working with Laura Bridgman. Extensive reading was excruciating due to her painful, weak eyes, but she was strong-minded and determined to make her own way in the world. With her mind resolved, she packed her few possessions and left for Alabama.

Thus began the great journey of two pioneers: the reluctant teacher and the stubborn student. Expectations were low all around. Many teachers had tried educating deaf and blind children since Dr. Howe first started working with Bridgman. All had failed. Furthermore, Mr. and Mrs. Keller had been told that their daughter was an imbecile. Although they believed she had some mental capacity, they were unable to communicate with her beyond the most basic level. Because of this, she had become very spoiled and unmanageable, acting more like a wild creature than an intelligent child.

Annie had an extremely difficult first month trying to connect with Helen. From the moment they met, Annie had been spelling words into Helen's hand. At first Helen could not comprehend the meaning of these gestures, and responded by imitating the finger motions like a bright, curious animal. Although the task must have seemed futile at times, Annie was extremely stubborn. She relentlessly spelled every part of Helen's day into her hand.

About one month after Annie's arrival, she finally connected with Helen. While Annie pumped water over Helen's hand, it suddenly came to Helen that the water she felt on one hand and the finger motions pressed into her other hand were uniquely related. All at once, she understood what Annie had been doing. Helen "asked" who this woman was that was dragging her into the civilized world literally kicking. "T-e-a-c-h-e-r" is what she was told. The mutual love and devotion that began at that moment would continue until Annie's death half a century later.

After realizing that Teacher had given her the means to join the world, Helen's progress was so rapid that educators everywhere became aware that a teacher perhaps even greater than Dr. Howe was at work. This teacher's gift was largely instinctive, as she had had only six years of formal education.

There were skeptics, however. Some attributed Helen's success to Annie's "interpretation" of what she said, since at first only Annie could communicate with her. An astute few realized that it was the combination of intuitive, gifted teacher and eager, intelligent pupil that produced such intriguing results. When Helen was twenty, she enrolled in Radcliffe College. Following the same curriculum as all the other young women, Helen graduated four years later *with honors*. Except for

Annie's presence as interpreter, Helen was given no special consideration.

Helen Keller and Annie Sullivan were almost constant companions and coworkers from their meeting in 1887 until Annie's death in 1936. They lived, worked, read, lectured, and traveled together. They even went on the vaudeville circuit at one point in an attempt to ease financial problems. When Annie married John Macy, a distinguished literary critic and scholar, he became part of their team.

Annie shared with Helen her passion for literature, for excellence in character and conversation, and a belief system that led Helen to consider herself an "ordinary" person. Annie believed that the greatest handicap faced by the disabled was the pity of others. Handicapped children had been treated as lesser life forms. She treated Helen exactly as she would a seeing and hearing child, with the one exception of spelling words into her hand instead of speaking them aloud. She was very demanding of Helen and would not allow anyone to pity or patronize her.

Annie wielded a great deal of power over Helen's scholastic and cultural world, especially in the early years. She could easily have abused that power. Instead she considered it a sacred trust. She made a vow to replace the blankness in Helen's life with intelligence, laughter, and independence.

Annie had quickly grown from someone reluctant to accept a potentially boring job into a self-sacrificing developer of a mind and soul too long neglected. Helen did not know until much later the extent of Annie's sacrifices. The extensive reading required at Radcliffe took a huge toll on her eyes. Often her eyes almost failed, and she needed numerous operations through the years in an effort to save her remaining sight. Doctors told her that it was unwise to the point of madness for her to read so much. Nearly every bit of her reading was done for Helen's benefit, and she refused to rest her eyes properly. Consequently, she spent many hours in pain and ultimately lost her eyesight completely.

Melancholy plagued Annie throughout her life, worsening as her eyesight failed. When a bout of depression struck, she disappeared until it was back under control. Sometimes she would even conceal herself for several hours under a boat on the shore in order to be alone. She always fought off her bleak thoughts within a day or two and refused to allow the gloominess into her relationships.

In 1931 Annie Sullivan was awarded a Doctor of Humane Letters degree from Temple University. She became known as one of the greatest contributors to the teaching of children – not just handicapped children. Dr. Maria Montessori called her a "true pioneer" in teaching methods.

A few weeks before her death on October 20, 1936, someone told her, "Teacher, you must get well. Without you, Helen would be nothing." Annie replied, "That would mean that I have failed." Annie knew that she had not failed. Clearly, she had honored her sacred trust. Helen continued to make her way successfully in the world. Of her beloved Teacher, she wrote, "She was lent to me from the Lord so that I might develop my own personality through darkness and silence. I can think of her only as a spirit giving out warmth, a sun of life."

There are many ways to be a partner of God. Annie Sullivan found her way, and the whole world watched in admiration. Prophets come from every walk of life, and they shout to the whole world something the world desperately needs to know. Can you think of any way that you could be a prophet, a partner of God?

14

Promise of Restoration

Dear Father, whom I cannot see,

I know that you are near to me.

Quite quietly I speak to you:

Please show me what you'd have me do.

Please help me plan kind things to do

For other people and for you.

Thank you for always helping me,

Dear Father, whom I cannot see.

– LILIAN COX

The town of Tekoa is a small village south of Jerusalem and south of Bethlehem. And it was from this village, on the edge of the Judean wilderness, that God called the first of the prophets. Suddenly, in the kingdom of Israel, the northern half of the divided kingdom of David, at the town of Bethel, the city that Jeroboam had set up as the religious rival of Jerusalem, there appeared a shepherd from Tekoa named

Amos, who spoke out against the immorality, cruelty, and paganism of this northern capital.

Amos was the beginning of the classical prophets of the Hebrew people, called to remind them again and again of their covenant with their God, and to promise God's blessing upon them if they returned to Him, and dire punishments if they continued in their ways. But the shepherd from Tekoa was immediately thrown out of the city and told that his prophecies were not welcome. "Everything is all right," they told him. "Why do you disturb us with your words of doom?"

But Amos's words were not words of doom, even though they prophesied that disaster would come to this northern kingdom if the people did not mend their ways. It was not their politics or their business dealings that the Lord was concerned about. It was those trivial matters that escape the attention of men and women intent on their own interests.

"They have rejected the Law of the Lord, and have not kept His statutes."

The northern kingdom had become a hotbed of injustice and high living, of neglect of the poor and oppression of the weak and helpless. Pride was everywhere – pride of family, pride of status, pride of wealth, and pride of political power. All the vices of a rich society abounded, and God was forgotten. And the warning came:

> Assemble on the hills of Samaria
> and observe the grave disorders inside her
> and the acts of oppression there.
> Little they know of right conduct...

They cram their palaces with violence and extortion.

That is why the Lord God says,

An enemy will besiege this land,

he will bring down your strength,

and your palaces will be looted.

– AMOS 3:9-11

But the prophet held out a promise of hope and restoration, that the king and his people would "do the right thing," return to their God, keep their covenant with Him, and turn from their evil ways. It was a promise that was fulfilled after the exile of the Jewish people to Babylon, when they were taught a hard lesson by their Lord and Creator:

Thus says the Lord, Behold the days are coming which the ploughman will overtake the reaper in his task, in which seed-time and vintage-time will be one. The mountainsides will flow with mud, and every hill will be cultivated. I will bring back my people, back from exile, to rebuild the deserted cities and dwell in them, plant vineyards and drink the wine of them, fence in gardens and eat their fruit. And I will settle them in their own land, never again shall they be torn away from it, this land which I have given them, says the Lord your God.

– AMOS 9:13-15

When we fail to do what is right, we have to face the consequences. Sometimes the consequences can be painful. But it is a Loving Father Who punishes. Once the lesson has been learned, He is more loving than before. That is the whole message of mercy and forgiveness.

ANNE FRANK

There are some persons whose great gift, in a dark age, is simply to maintain a candlelight of humanity and so to guarantee that darkness should not have the final word. Anne Frank, a Jewish child who perished during the Holocaust, was surely one of these. Her life was extinguished at the age of fifteen – thus contributing to the Nazi dream of a Jewish-free Europe. But her light continued to burn, thus fulfilling her own dream: "I want to go on living after my death."

Anne's story is well known. She was born on June 12, 1929. During the Nazi occupation of Holland, her family and another family, the Van Daams, took shelter in a "secret annex" in her father's office in the center of Amsterdam. They remained sequestered for two years. Keeping still all day, never able to leave their hidden quarters, they relied on the support of Dutch friends to preserve their secret, to bring them supplies and news of the outside world. Anne was thirteen when she entered the annex in July 1942. Besides her schoolbooks and her treasured scrapbook of Hollywood stars, Anne brought along with her a diary she had received for her thirteenth birthday. Addressing her daily entries to an imaginary girlfriend, "Kitty," Anne faithfully kept her diary throughout the course of her captivity. This diary was published after the war and was quickly acclaimed as one of the most deeply affecting artifacts of the Holocaust. But because of Anne's unusual gifts as a writer and because of the extraordinary qualities of her personality, her work merits recognition as a literary classic in its own right and as one of the great moral documents of the twentieth century.

For Anne herself keeping a diary was not simply a distraction but a duty, a responsibility to render her experience and her feelings in the most accurate possible terms. "I want to write, but more than that, I want to bring out all kinds of things that lie buried deep in my heart," she writes in the early pages. With remarkable skill Anne manages to describe the personalities and atmosphere in the annex – the strain of captivity and close quarters and the brave efforts to carry on with life. All this takes place against a backdrop of fear and the constant danger of discovery.

> "I see the eight of us with our 'Secret Annex' as if we were a little piece of blue heaven, surrounded by heavy black rain clouds. The round, clearly defined spot where we stand is still safe, but the clouds gather more closely about us and the circle which separates us from the approaching danger closes more and more tightly."

The diary is mostly a sharply recorded chronicle of the everyday trials and the modest joys of a young girl's

life "underground." But it also contains Anne's remark-
ably unchildlike reflections on the meaning of life and
faith in the face of adversity.

> "The best remedy for those who are afraid, lone-
> ly, or unhappy is to go outside, somewhere where
> they can be quiet alone with the heavens, nature,
> and God. Because only then does one feel that all
> is as it should be and that God wishes to see peo-
> ple happy, amidst the simple beauty of nature. As
> long as this exists...I know that there will always
> be comfort for every sorrow, whatever the cir-
> cumstances may be."

Lying in bed, she says she ends her evening prayers
with the words, "I thank you, God, for all that is good
and dear and beautiful," and adds, "I am filled with joy...
I don't think of all the misery, but of the beauty that still
remains."

Aside from acknowledging the terror that prowls
beyond her hiding place, the diary also reflects the mys-
terious unfolding of Anne's personality, her emergence
from childhood, and her growing sense of herself as a
person with a future and a task in the world.

> "I know what I want, I have a goal, an opinion, I
> have a religion and love. Let me be myself and
> then I am satisfied. I know that I am a woman, a
> woman with inward strength and plenty of
> courage. If God lets me live...I shall not remain
> insignificant, I shall work in the world and for

mankind! And now I know that first and foremost
I shall require courage and cheerfulness."

Rarely has anyone so well defined the virtues
required by our age – "courage and cheerfulness" – as
this fourteen-year-old girl already living under sentence
of death.

In August 1944, soon after Anne's fifteenth birthday,
the secret annex was betrayed and all its eight inhabitants were dispersed among the factories of death. Only
Otto Frank, Anne's father, survived the war and
returned to the old house in Amsterdam. He learned
that his wife had died in January 1945 in Auschwitz,
while Anne and her sister Margot had died of typhus in
Bergen-Belsen in early March. Then he was presented
with the diaries of his daughter, lovingly preserved by
friends in hopes of her eventual return.

In light of her death, it is excruciating to read Anne's
intimate confidences, her account of the homey details
of life in hiding. But through the girlish record of quar-
rels with her mother, worries about her studies, and the
possibilities for finding romantic happiness with the Van
Daams' teenage son, Otto Frank was the first to recognize in his daughter's diary a profound witness to the
value of life and the virtue of hope. Words written days
before her arrest only gain additional power in the light
of her fate:

> "In spite of everything I still believe that people
> are really good at heart... I see the world gradu-
> ally being turned into a wilderness, I hear the

ever-approaching thunder, which will destroy us too, I can feel the sufferings of millions and yet, if I look up into the heavens, I think that it will all come right... In the meantime, I must uphold my ideals, for perhaps the time will come when I shall be able to carry them out."

Sometimes we show that we are prophets by the way we face difficulties, or even death. Anne Frank is one of the great prophets of our time. Can you tell why? What does her life say? What great truths and qualities did she witness?

MARIAN ANDERSON

Contralto Marian Anderson was the first black American to become a permanent member of the Metropolitan Opera Company and the first black American to perform at the White House. In 1939, the Daughters of the American Revolution, who owned Constitution Hall, forbade her to sing there, which caused Eleanor Roosevelt to resign her membership in the DAR and schedule a concert for Marian Anderson on the steps of the Lincoln Memorial.

She had a voice that dazzled Toscanini and a dedication that heartened the whole world. Marian Anderson, who died in 1993 at the age of ninety-six, sang compellingly that her Lord held the whole world in His hands. With her gloriously quiet manner, she, too, held multitudes in her hands.

142

When a benighted nation tried to keep her back because of her race, Marian Anderson replied with beautiful song, not loud rage. She converted white bigots' hatred into artistic energy. And she laid claim on the consciences of decent Americans, easing the way for recognition of other black Americans, artists and nonartists.

It was many Easter Sundays ago that Marian Anderson sang to seventy-five thousand people at the Lincoln Memorial because the Daughters of the American Revolution had denied her their hall. She was civilly obedient, willing to let her deep and delicate contralto answer the libels on her race. Past her prime when she reached the stage of the Metropolitan Opera, she still mustered a haunting Ulrica in Verdi's *Un Ballo in Maschera*.

To hear Marian Anderson sing in person was to marvel not only at her vocal mastery but also at the total focus of the singer on her art, shutting out the world as though she hadn't shaken it with her achievements. What a sound, what a presence, what a moment for American music!

How was Marian Anderson a prophetic voice for African-Americans against racism in the United States? Can you name other singers and artists for whom she paved the way?

Being Faithful in Bad Times

Bring to fruition, Creator God,

the work of Your kingdom.

Make us part of that joyful harvest

in which Your loving purpose is completed.

Help us to realize

how important the smallest words and deeds are

in the context of eternity.

At harvest time, when we remember Your goodness,

make us grateful also

for all we have received from the labor of others

who have sown the seeds of faith, hope and love in

   our lives.

– AUTHOR UNKNOWN

It is a temptation for those who believe in God to wonder where He is at times. There seems to be no profit in serving Him. If we look around, we observe that those who don't believe in Him seem to prosper. We may wonder what use it is to serve God and keep His commandments when those who ignore Him and do evil seem to be well off.

The prophets ask if you will be faithful to God only in good times, or if you will also be faithful when things are falling apart. What is important is fidelity to God and to our own conscience. There will always be those who are faithful only when things are going well. That is the problem the prophet Malachi was facing.

Malachi is the last of the classical prophets. His book was written after the Jewish people had returned to Judah from their exile in Babylon. The temple had been rebuilt, and Ezra, one of the great leaders of the return, had just begun his reform. But things were not quite right with God's people. Malachi began by telling them about God's undying love for them. Should they not respond like dutiful children to their Father? "Look to yourselves," the prophet told them, "and give to God the honor that is due to Him."

The great reform of the Jewish religion and temple worship under Ezra was still in its beginning stages, and there was much confusion about exactly what it meant to be a Jew. The walls of Jerusalem had scarcely been rebuilt, and the population of the holy city was still very small. All kinds of pagan practices had begun to creep in, and the commandments of God were not clearly known.

The following scene from the Book of Nehemiah, one of the most dramatic in the whole Bible, had just taken place.

> "When the seventh month came round…all the people gathered in the square in front of the Water Gate, and asked the scribe Ezra to bring the Book of the Law of Moses which God had prescribed for Israel… In the presence of the men and women, and those old enough to understand, he read from the book from dawn till noon, and all the people listened attentively.
>
> Ezra read from the Book of the Law, translating and giving the meaning, so the reading was understood… In the full view of all the people… Ezra opened the book… The people were in tears as they listened to the words of the Law… Then all of the people went off to eat and drink…and enjoy themselves…since they had understood the meaning of what had been proclaimed to them.
>
> – NEHEMIAH 8:1-3, 8, 9, 12

And here began the great scribal tradition, which would preserve the holy books through the centuries. The words of Moses and the prophets were carefully preserved, and the writing craft began. These great scrolls were read week after week in the synagogues and in the temple, so that the Jewish nation would never forget their history and the words of their God.

We read the word of God with the same reverence, and if we follow that teaching, the blessings promised by the prophets will fall upon us as well.

BEETHOVEN'S TRIUMPH

As a child, Ludwig van Beethoven could play the piano better than most adults. He gave his first public concert when he was only seven years old; at age eleven, he worked as an organist at the Court of Cologne; at twelve he published his first significant composition. Four years later he visited Vienna and played for the great Mozart, who afterward left the room saying, "Watch that boy! Someday he will make the world talk about him."

Ludwig's father, who was a singer at the Court, had visions of making piles of gold by charging people to hear his "wonder child." It seems he thought more about the money – and the drink it could buy – than he did about Ludwig's happiness. He used to reel into the house in the early hours of the morning, haul the sleepy boy from bed to piano, and conduct forced lessons until dawn, never sparing a few knocks and blows when the exhausted child missed a note.

It is a wonder that his father's harshness did not make Ludwig hate all music. Perhaps it was his gentle mother who helped him keep his courage through those troubling times. But when Ludwig was seventeen, his mother died. His father at once sold her clothes so he could buy more drink.

Ludwig felt the loss deeply. Now there was no one to take care of his two younger brothers. Taking matters into his own hands, he asked the prince to pay him half his father's salary so he could support his brothers. His request was granted, his father's career at the Court came to an end, and Ludwig became the head of the family. For the rest of his life he looked after his brothers, even though they often got into trouble and caused him more than enough anguish.

In 1792, when he was not quite twenty-two years old, Ludwig moved to Vienna to study under Joseph Haydn, the most famous living composer. Those years in Vienna were filled with hard work. He learned to play many instruments. He studied the horn, viola, violin, and clarinet, so he would better know how to write music for the orchestra. He labored over his scores, writing, correcting, revising, rejecting, and starting over again.

Gradually, the word of his genius spread. The citizens of Vienna were a music-loving people. Whenever they could, they flocked to hear Beethoven play. He gave a series of concerts in 1795, one of them for the benefit of Mozart's widow and children. From then on, his success seemed assured. For the next several years he wrote, and traveled, and performed, and made himself into a truly great musician.

Then, sometime before he was twenty-eight years old, he began to notice a humming in his ears. At first he tried to ignore it, but it only grew worse and worse.

Finally, reluctantly, he consulted doctors. Their diagnosis was worse than a sentence of death: Beethoven was going deaf.

For a long time he could not bear to tell anyone. He shunned all company. "I confess I am living a wretched life," he wrote to a friend. "For two years I have avoided almost all social gatherings because it is impossible for me to say to people, 'I am deaf.' If I belonged to another profession, it would be easier…"

He found refuge in the country, where he could take long walks alone through the woods. "My deafness troubles me less here than elsewhere," he wrote. "Every tree seems to speak to me of God."

Convinced he was going to die, Beethoven confessed his shame and despair in a testament he meant to leave behind for his brothers. "I could not bring myself to say to people, 'Speak louder, shout, for I am deaf'," he wrote. "How should I bring myself to admit the weakness of a sense which ought to be more perfect in me than in others, a sense which I once possessed in the greatest perfection?… I must live like an exile. If I venture into company a burning dread falls on me, the dreadful risk of letting my condition be perceived… What humiliation when someone stood by me and heard a flute in the distance, and I heard *nothing,* or when someone heard the herdboy singing, and I again heard nothing. Such occurrences brought me near to despair, a little more and I had put an end to my own life…"

And yet Beethoven did something much more courageous than give up. He gave himself to his art. He went on writing music, even though what he wrote grew fainter and fainter in his own ears. As his hearing faded, his music began to take on a quality much different from the elegant compositions written by earlier composers. Many of Beethoven's works grew stormy and emotional and thrilling – much like his own courageous and turbulent life. Strange and wonderful to say, he wrote much of his best music, the music we remember him for, after he lost his ability to hear.

Eventually Beethoven went completely deaf. He was lonely and often unhappy, and yet he managed to compose uplifting music. His last symphony, the Ninth, concludes with the famous *Ode to Joy.* When the work was complete, Beethoven agreed to conduct an orchestra and choir in a concert in Vienna.

The hall was packed. Beethoven took his place in the center of the orchestra, with his back to the audience, and at a signal from him the music began. The magnificent strains entranced the audience. Yet Beethoven himself heard nothing. He followed the score only in his mind. The musicians had been directed to watch him, but to pay not a bit of attention to his beating of the time.

When it was over, the great master lowered his arms. He stood amid the silence, fumbling with his score. One of the singers tugged at his sleeve and motioned him to look. Beethoven turned around.

He saw people on their feet, clapping their hands, waving their hats, throwing their arms into the air. The deaf musician bowed, and every eye in the audience held a tear.

The final years of this great soul's life were sad. During his last illness he found great comfort in reading music. A friend sent him some of Haydn's compositions, and he passed many pleasant hours going over the notes. He found much comfort, too, in Schubert's Songs. He died in 1827, and it is said that among his final words were these: "I shall hear in heaven."

God calls each one of us to accomplish something unique and original. Beethoven listened to his inner voice, his own "prophetic" instinct, and despite great suffering, he made great music. What voice do you hear inside you? What obstacles will you have to overcome to accomplish it? Can you see where the providence of God is leading you?

16

Worship God Sincerely

Dear God,

Help me to take the right path in life and

Help me to know right from wrong.

Show me the way to get through life and its problems

No matter how hard they are.

Help me to build a life I can be proud of and

Show me the way to make a happy life.

I put my trust in You as You are a God Who loves

Us no matter who we are.

– CRAIG ADAMS

Besides the discovery of the books of the law, which so electrified the children of Israel after their return from Babylon, the next great effort was to rebuild the temple and the dignity of public worship. The Jewish people were constantly tempted to worship the gods of their neighbors. With the temple in ruins, the temptation was even greater.

The rebuilding of the temple took much labor and a long time. According to the detailed prescriptions in the holy books, the proper worship of God had to be restored, yet there were no priests trained to carry on this worship.

It was the heart of worship to offer the best gifts to the Lord: the first fruits, unblemished lambs, the best heifers. They were to give all that was expressive of their devotion to the Creator.

But that was not being done, and Malachi, along with the prophets Haggai and Zechariah, spoke out against the laxity of the worshipers and the carelessness of the priests. Malachi prophesied that in the future a pure worship would be offered to God in every time and place, beginning in Jerusalem: "From farthest east to farthest west, My Name will be great among the nations, and everywhere incense and a pure gift will be offered to My Name, for My Name will be great among the nations."

Zechariah went even further. His words sound like a scene from the New Testament:

> Rejoice heart and soul, daughter Zion!
> Shout for joy, daughter of Jerusalem!
> Look, your king is approaching,
> He is vindicated and victorious,
> Humble and riding on a donkey,
> On a colt, the foal of a donkey.
> …He will proclaim peace to the nations,
> His empire will stretch from sea to sea,

From the river to the ends of the earth.

– ZECHARIAH 9:9-10

While urging them to return to the covenant of their fathers, the prophets said in substance that the best is yet to come, that the time would come when the Lord would say to His people, "Do I need the blood of goats and heifers? Do you think that I am hungry and need something to eat? What I desire is a contrite and humbled heart. *That* is the sacrifice that I desire."

What began with the return of the exiles from Babylon was an educational process: to teach God's people of their true calling as His cherished children, who had been given His law and His revelation, and to urge them to be worthy of their bond with Him. This was the beginning of Second Temple Judaism, when the temple was once again the center of Jewish worship. This was a time when synagogues were built in every small town and village, when scribes were trained to pass on the sacred scrolls of the covenant, and when the great feasts of Passover, Shavuot, and Sukkoth were once again celebrated.

"Your joy is in your God," the people were told. "This is the beginning and end of your salvation and your security." After the words of Malachi, the prophets were silent, and the people had only the words written on the scrolls to remind them of God's commandments. Those scrolls were studied, copied, and taught until the coming of Jesus of Nazareth, five hundred years later.

"See that you keep holy the Lord's Day" is still a solemn commandment. How do you take part in worship? Do you give your Creator the best of your time and attention? Do you understand what genuine worship is really all about? What could help you to understand worship better?

OSKAR SCHINDLER

If the Holocaust represents the mystery of iniquity, then the story of Oskar Schindler, born on April 28, 1908, may be said to represent the mystery of goodness. The mystery in his case is not simply why he did his good work of rescuing Jews from the Nazis while others did not. The mystery is also why he did this good work. For, noble as his deeds undoubtedly were, they appeared oddly out of character with everything else about the man.

Schindler was a German industrialist who recognized in the war and particularly in the Nazi occupation of Poland a lucrative business opportunity. In Cracow he established an enamel-goods factory employing Jewish workers from the ghetto. In the beginning there was little to distinguish Schindler from many similar entrepreneurs. Over time, however, it became clear that this was no ordinary German factory. It was a haven, an oasis of life. Those lucky enough to be assigned to Schindler's factory were preserved under a unique canopy of protection from the raging storm of annihilation.

Even while he lavished "unnecessary" food and resources on his workers, Schindler still managed to make his fortune. But as the Nazis tightened their noose around the Jews, Schindler's occupation steadily

156

changed. Before long the rescue and preservation of "his Jews" became, in fact, his only real business. Running a factory was simply a pretext for saving lives.

To this end he bargained, cajoled, bribed, and even gambled to win concessions from his Nazi "friends" – anything to widen the tenuous circle of life. At every step there was the danger that he would go too far, that he would call too much attention to his enterprise of mercy and thus jeopardize everything. Twice he was arrested by the Gestapo and interrogated – the first time, after he was denounced for having kissed one of his Jewish employees. In both cases highly placed friends vouched for him and won his release. But rather than retreat, each threat of personal danger served simply to embolden him in his single-minded crusade.

The most audacious venture came toward the end of the war. With the rising prospect of Nazi defeat, Polish factories began to close. Their labor no longer needed, Jewish workers were simply fed into the ovens of Auschwitz. Schindler won permission to transfer his entire workforce of eleven hundred men, women, and children to a new site in Czechoslovakia. When the train carrying the women was inadvertently diverted to Auschwitz Schindler raced to the camp, armed with a sack of diamonds and gold, to win their rescue. His new factory, ostensibly devoted to weapons production, was actually an enormous confidence game. Though guarded by SS troops and run with apparent efficiency, the factory produced nothing. Schindler was determined not to

contribute in any way to the Nazi war effort. While waiting out the end of the war he spent his entire savings to
keep the factory in operation, all the time managing to
convince the Nazis of his industry and good faith.

Finally, in May 1945 the war ended. The guards fled,
shamed by Schindler into disobeying their orders to
exterminate the surviving workers. Within hours of the
armistice, Schindler and his wife also fled, disguised in
the uniforms of camp inmates, lest he be captured and
lynched as a German industrialist. The prisoners sent
him off in an emotional ceremony. They presented
Oskar with a ring, fashioned from gold dental work
which was donated by one of the grateful prisoners.
Inscribed on the ring were words from the Talmud: "He
who saves one life saves the entire world."

No one, least of all "Schindler's Jews," doubts that
what he did was an unqualified good. But no one is quite
sure *why* he did it. His Catholic upbringing is no expla-
nation; he never seems to have had any religious
impulse. He was an opportunist and profiteer, a gambler, a drinker, and a faithless husband. Arguably it was
precisely the fact that he was the last man anyone would
suspect of heroism that allowed him to get away with it.
Still the mystery remains. From somewhere in the
depths of his own morally complicated character
Schindler found the resources to wage a private contest
with the devil. The mystery of Schindler is a reminder
of the audacity that distinguishes genuine heroism from
merely conventional virtue, goodness, or even piety.

Schindler survived the postwar chaos, though he was totally impoverished by his wartime enterprise. He never again found a métier for his unusual talents. But as his story became more widely known he was inducted into the list of the Righteous Gentiles in Israel. When he died in October 1974, he was buried, according to his request, in Jerusalem.

Oskar Schindler's gift of prophecy was not in words, but in deeds. He risked his life to save others. What does Jesus say about this kind of heroism? How is this kind of compassion prophecy?

On January 13, 1982, Air Florida Flight 90 struck the 14th Street Bridge after taking off from Washington, D.C.'s National Airport, and plunged into the icy Potomac River, killing seventy-eight people. Hundreds of commuters, heading home early because of a rare Washington blizzard, stood on the river's banks and watched torturous rescue attempts. Following is a newspaper report of one such courageous rescue.

LENNY SKUTNIK

Lenny Skutnik, who dove into the ice-choked Potomac River Wednesday to save the life of a drowning woman following the jetliner crash in the Potomac, has had little experience in the hero business.

Skutnik, 28, whose full name is Martin Leonard Skutnik III, is experienced in less exalted matters. He's been a meat-packer, house painter, furniture-plant worker, hamburger cook, and strip-and-wax man at Ralph's Supermarket in Simi Valley, California.

Skutnik now works for the Congressional Budget Office, where he runs errands, delivers mail and makes $14,000 a year. A big night out, Skutnik says, is taking his wife, Linda, and their two sons to Brothers Pizza near their $325-a-month rented town house in Lorton, Virginia. "Every once in a while we'll close our eyes and blow a couple of bucks," he says.

The only other time in his life that he had a chance to be a hero, Skutnik says, he flubbed it. He was anchoring a relay team in a high school race and he could have won the race, but he pooped out and stopped. The coach yelled at him: "You quit, Skutnik. You quit."

Late Wednesday afternoon, as one of hundreds of homeward-bound commuters drawn to the banks of the Potomac by the crash of Air Florida Flight 90, Skutnik, who's never taken a life-saving course, saved a woman who was too weak to grasp rescue rings lowered from a hovering helicopter. Television spread pictures of his valor to the nation.

President Reagan, in a speech in New York, spoke of Skutnik's bravery: "Nothing had picked him out particularly to be a hero, but without hesitation there he was and he saved her life."

Interviewed yesterday at his home twenty miles south of the 14th Street bridge, Skutnik could offer no fancy explanations for risking his life. "Nobody else was doing anything," he said. "It was the only way."

The woman Skutnik rescued apparently was Priscilla Tirado, whose husband and infant son perished in the crash. After the rescue, as he waited in an ambulance that had run out of blankets, Skutnik gave his coat to Joseph Stiley, a survivor of the crash who had two broken legs and was shivering. Shirtless and shivering himself, Skutnik, who lost his watch and a cap in the river, was taken to National Hospital for Orthopedics and Rehabilitation in Arlington for treatment of hypothermia. He didn't want to go.

"I'd heard all these horror stories about hospitals and all the forms. The first thing I said when I got there was, 'Is this going to cost me anything?'" said Skutnik, who's described by his colleagues at CBO as an exemplary worker.

He was dispatched, free of charge, to a hot tub in the hospital to soak for forty minutes and warm up. When Skutnik got out of the tub, he faced reporters – scores of them, frenzied and facing deadlines. They pushed and shoved to ask him what "it felt like." He had never met a reporter before. He told his story again and again.

Skutnik's instant celebrity began Wednesday afternoon near the 14th Street bridge when traffic in the express lane he was car-pooling home in came to an abrupt stop. Skutnik followed scores of stalled commuters down to the river, where there was a rumor that someone had been hurt. He said he didn't hear the metallic crash of the plane and the bridge.

From the shore, Skutnik said he saw the partially submerged plane with a half dozen passengers clinging to it. He saw one spectator tie a rope around his waist and attempt a rescue.

The man who tried to swim out to the wreckage was Roger Olian, 34, a sheet metal worker from Arlington, who was drawn to the accident after getting caught in traffic near the bridge on his way home from work.

"I went in with a makeshift rope that kept getting stuck on the ice," Olian said yesterday. "I was about five feet from the plane when the helicopters arrived. But by then I'd just about had it. I nearly sank, but they pulled me in," said Olian.

Later, when it became obvious that a helicopter could not save the drowning woman, Skutnik said he didn't have any profound thoughts. "I just did it," he said. "When I got out of the water, I was satisfied. I did what I set out to do."

Prophets come in many forms, and Lenny Skutnik was a special kind of prophet. He set out to do what was right, and soon the whole world was watching. But he did what was right because it was right. This told the whole world something. What did he tell the world? Would you have done the same thing if you had been in his place?

Do Not Wish Evil

Blessed are you, O Lord our God,

King of the universe!

At Your word night falls.

In Your wisdom You open heaven's gates,

You control the elements and rotate the seasons.

You set the stars in the vault of heaven.

You created night and day.

You cause the light to fade when darkness comes

And the darkness to melt away in the light of the new
    day.

O ever-living God,

You will always watch over us, Your creatures.

Blessed are You, O Lord,

At whose word night falls.

– A JEWISH PRAYER

Sometimes prophecies come in the form of stories, like the story of the Good Samaritan or the Prodigal Son in the New Testament. The book of Jonah is also a story about the danger of hatred and the desire to punish one's enemies. It was written when the empire of Assyria was a great danger to the Jewish people and there was hatred in the hearts of everyone and a wish for the destruction of their enemies.

In the story, Jonah is symbolic of the Hebrew people, or of anyone who looks to the destruction of his or her enemies. God sent a Hebrew prophet to a pagan people, a pagan city, not only different from the Jewish people, but also their mortal enemy, worshiping a different god and living contrary to the commandments that had been given to Israel.

Jonah was indignant at the command to preach repentance to a foreign and idolatrous people. In order to escape from the mission given to him by God, he boarded a ship going in the opposite direction of the city to which he was sent.

But the God who sent him on his mission is the Lord of wind and wave and ocean. God sent a great storm, threatening the vessel and everyone on it. When the crew of the ship discovered that Jonah had made God angry, they threw him overboard. The storm subsided, and Jonah was brought to the place God sent him to – in the belly of a whale.

The truth behind the story is that God has compassion for the people of every nation and culture, since He is the Creator of all. And Jonah found himself forced to carry out his mission in spite of himself. He went to Nineveh, the capital of the Assyrian empire, on the Tigris River. The story of Jonah is a parable about political plots and military exploits in the name of national pride. God's providence extends to the people of all nations.

This is still a powerful lesson today, when "ethnic cleansing" and racial hatred are the seeds of war and the reason for war. It is often the reason for gangs in our cities and towns, and for the violence and murder that gangs take part in. Like Jonah, we don't like to be told that we must love and respect those who are different from us. Like Jonah, we sometimes have to be taught this lesson by a God who commands us to love our neighbors, and even our enemies, as ourselves.

In July, 1963, while the Battle of Gettysburg was going on, Confederate raider, John Hunt Morgan, a Kentuckian, led a cavalry into Ohio. That is the setting of this poem.

KENTUCKY BELLE

Summer of 'sixty-three, sir, and Conrad was
     gone away –
Gone to the country town, sir, to sell our first
     load of hay.
We lived in the log house yonder, poor as ever
     you've seen;
Roschen there was a baby, and I was only nine-
     teen.

Conrad, he took the oxen, but he left Kentucky
     Belle;
How much we thought of Kentuck, I couldn't
     begin to tell –

Came from the Bluegrass country; my father
    gave her to me
When I rode north with Conrad, away from
    Tennessee.

Conrad lived in Ohio – a German he is, you
    know –
The house stood in broad cornfields, stretching
    on, row after row;
The old folks made me welcome; they were kind
    as kind could be;
But I kept longing, longing, for the hills of
    Tennessee.

O, for a sight of water, the shadowed slope of a
    hill!
Clouds that hang on the summit, a wind that is
    never still!
But the level land went stretching away to meet
    the sky –
Never a rise, from north to south, to rest the
    weary eye!

From east to west, no river to shine out under
    the moon,
Nothing to make a shadow in the yellow after-
    noon;
Only the breathless sunshine, as I looked out, all
    forlorn,
Only the "rustle, rustle," as I walked among the
    corn.

When I fell sick with pining we didn't wait any
    more,
But moved away from the cornlands out to this
    river shore –
The Tuscarawas it's called, sir – off there's a hill,
    you see –
And now I've grown to like it next best to the
    Tennessee.

I was at work that morning. Someone came rid-
    ing like mad
Over the bridge and up the road – Farmer
    Rouf's little lad.
Bareback he rode; he had no hat; he hardly
    stopped to say,
"Morgan's men are coming, Frau, they're gallop-
    ing on this way.

"I'm sent to warn the neighbors. He isn't a mile
    behind;
He sweeps up all the horses – every horse that
    he can find;
Morgan, Morgan the raider, and Morgan's terri-
    ble men,
With bowie knives and pistols, are galloping up
    the glen."

The lad rode down the valley, and I stood still at
    the door –
The baby laughed and prattled, playing with
    spools on the floor;

Kentuck was out in the pasture; Conrad, my
    man, was gone;
Near, near Morgan's men were galloping, gallop-
    ing on!

Sudden I picked up baby and ran to the pasture
    bar:
"Kentuck!" I called; "Kentucky!" She knew me
    ever so far!
I led her down the gully that turns off there to
    the right,
And tied her to the bushes; her head just out of
    sight.

As I ran back to the log house at once there
    came a sound –

The ring of hoofs, galloping hoofs, trembling
    over the ground,
Coming into the turnpike out from the White-
    Woman Glen –
Morgan, Morgan the raider, and Morgan's terri-
    ble men.

As near they drew and nearer my heart beat fast
    in alarm;
But still I stood in the doorway, with baby on my
    arm.
They came; they passed; with spur and whip in
    haste they sped along;

Morgan, Morgan the raider, and his band six
hundred strong.
Weary they looked and jaded, riding through
night and through day;
Pushing on east to the river, many long miles
away,
To the border strip where Virginia runs up into
the west,
And for the Upper Ohio before they could stop
to rest.

On like the wind they hurried, and Morgan rode
in advance;
Bright were his eyes like live coals, as he gave
me a sideways glance;
And I was just breathing freely, after my choking
pain,
When the last one of the troopers suddenly drew
his rein.

Frightened I was to death, sir; I scarce dared
look in his face,
As he asked for a drink of water and glanced
around the place;
I gave him a cup, and he smiled – 'twas only a
boy, you see,

Faint and worn, with dim blue eyes, and he'd
sailed on the Tennessee.

Only sixteen, he was, sir – a fond mother's only
    son –
Off and away with Morgan before his life had
    begun!
The damp drops stood on his temples; drawn
    was the boyish mouth;
And I thought me of the mother waiting down in
    the South!

O, pluck was he to the backbone and clear grit
    through and through;
Boasted and bragged like a trooper, but the big
    words wouldn't do;
The boy was dying, sir, dying, as plain as plain
    could be,
Worn out by his ride with Morgan up from the
    Tennessee.

But, when I told the laddie that I too was from
    the South,
Water came in his dim blue eyes and quivers
    around his mouth.
"Do you know the Bluegrass country?" he wist-
    ful began to say,
Then swayed like a willow sapling and fainted
    dead away.

I had him into the log house, and worked and
    brought him to;
I fed him and coaxed him, as I thought his moth-
    er'd do;

And, when the lad got better, and the noise in
    his head was gone,
Morgan's men were miles away, galloping, gal-
    loping on.

"O, I must go," he muttered; "I must be up and
    away!
Morgan, Morgan is waiting for me! O, what will
    Morgan say?"
But I heard a sound of tramping and kept him
    back from the door –
The ringing sound of horses' hoofs that I had
    heard before.

And on, on came the soldiers – the Michigan
    cavalry –
And fast they rode, and black they looked gallop-
    ing rapidly;
They had followed hard on Morgan's track; they
    had followed day and night;
But of Morgan and Morgan's raiders they had
    never caught a sight.

And rich Ohio sat startled through all those
    summer days,
For strange, wild men were galloping over her
    broad highways;
Now here, now there, now seen, now gone, now
    north, now east, now west,
Through river valleys and corn-land farms,
    sweeping away her best.

A bold ride and a long ride! But they were taken
    at last.
They almost reached the river by galloping hard
    and fast;
But the boys in blue were upon them ere ever
    they gained the ford,
And Morgan, Morgan the raider, laid down his
    terrible sword.

Well, I kept the boy till evening – kept him
    against his will –
But he was too weak to follow, and sat there pale
    and still;
When it was cool and dusky – you'll wonder to
    hear me tell –
But I stole down to that gully and brought up
    Kentucky Belle.

I kissed the star on her forehead – my pretty,
    gentle lass –
But I knew that she'd be happy back in the old
    Bluegrass;
A suit of clothes of Conrad's, with all the money
    I had,
And Kentuck, pretty Kentuck, I gave to the
    worn-out lad.

I guided him to the southward as well as I knew
    how;

The boy rode off with many thanks, and many a
    backward bow;
And then the glow it faded, and my heart began
    to swell,
As down the glen away she went, my lost
    Kentucky Belle!

When Conrad came home in the evening the
    moon was shining high;
Baby and I were both crying – I couldn't tell him
    why –
But a battered suit of rebel gray was hanging on
    the wall,
And a thin old horse with a drooping head stood
    in Kentucky's stall.

Well, he was kind, and never once said a hard
    word to me;
He knew I couldn't help it – 'twas all for the
    Tennessee;
But, after the war was over, just think what came
    to pass –
A letter, sir; and the two were safe back in the
    old Bluegrass.

The lad had got across the border, riding
    Kentucky Belle;
And Kentuck, she was thriving, and fat, and
    hearty, and well;

He cared for her, and kept her, nor touched her
    with whip or spur;
Ah! we've had many horses, but never a horse
    like her!

This is a story of bravery under fire, of refusing to give in to fear and panic. We have bonds with everyone, sometimes stronger than those of blood and kinship. This woman put aside her fears for herself and helped someone in trouble, even though helping that someone was dangerous. In what way is this story like the prophecies of Jonah? What lesson does it teach you?

CHAPTER 18

Sin and Repentance

Give me a candle of the Spirit, O God,

As I go down into the depths of my being.

Show me the hidden things, the creatures of

    my dreams,

The storehouse of forgotten memories and hurts.

Take me down to the spring of my life

And tell me my nature and my name.

Give me freedom to grow, so that I may become

    that self,

That seed of which You planted in me at my making.

Out of the depths, I cry to You, O God.

– GEORGE APPLETON

The prophet is a person, not a microphone. Prophets do not just mouth commandments and warnings. They confront situations with real people who are caught in a web of their own making. Their mission is sometimes painful and hazardous, yet they have to bring the mind of God to bear upon a situation that has happened because of the malice, stupidity, or greed that crops up in the human heart. Their mission is to change hearts. They do this, first of all, through detailed knowledge of the people and situations they are facing.

The aim of the prophetic mission is repentance and turning from behavior that displeases God. If the present behavior is headed for disaster, it is the work of the prophet to avert this disaster by evoking striking images through powerful words.

Sin is bad behavior, immoral behavior, irresponsible behavior, which is displeasing to God. He has made clear the kind of behavior that is unacceptable to Him. Genuine repentance starts with the realization that we have done wrong and must change.

Some habits of sin become deeply rooted, and thus are very difficult to change. That is where we are assured that we are not alone in the effort. Habits of sin destroy us, sap us of spiritual energy, and plunge us into a world of self-destruction. Some of us are like the Prodigal Son that Jesus speaks of in the Gospel: We run away from our true home and abandon ourselves to human weakness.

Our bad behavior has consequences, sometimes terrible and terrifying. All we have to do is look around us to see people who have wasted their lives by cultivating terrible weaknesses and behaviors they are unwilling to change. Self-destruction becomes a way of life.

Jonah was sent to a wicked city, where every kind of evil was cultivated. He was told to preach to the inhabitants and to bring them to repentance. He did not want to do this because he was sure that once they repented, God would forgive them and his warnings would be a waste of time. He was angry with God for forgiving – a strange attitude in a prophet.

We have to make sure that God's words to us do not go unheeded. We should look carefully at our behavior to see that it is in keeping with God's law. Our prophets are our parents and our teachers, our priests, ministers, and rabbis: those who bring the word of God to us.

"Turn away from evil, and do good," is still what the voice of the prophet cries out.

MARTIN NIEMOELLER

In the 1920s, Martin Niemoeller wrote a successful autobiography entitled *From U-boat to Pulpit.* In the light of the constant testing of his Christian conscience it was necessary in successive editions to revise that title so that it might finally read *From U-boat to Pulpit to Prison to Pacifism.*

Niemoeller had served as a highly decorated German U-boat commander during World War I. The casualty rate for U-Boat crews was so high that all who survived were revered as exceptional heroes. Like many German officers Niemoeller regarded the war's loss with a deep sense of betrayal, exacerbated by the humiliating terms of the Versailles treaty. Though after the war he decided to pursue his father's career as a Lutheran pastor, he maintained the hope that Germany would one day realize its intended greatness. In such a frame of mind he was an early supporter of National Socialism, believing in Hitler's promise to vindicate German honor.

Nevertheless, within months of Hitler's rise to power in 1933, Niemoeller had begun to feel uneasy with the hateful extremism of the Nazis. He was further disedified by the emergence of the so-called German Christian movement, which virtually identified the gospel with the Nazi ideology. Many distinguished church leaders and theologians felt no such qualms, and Niemoeller began to attract controversy. At first his principal concern was to maintain the independence and freedom of the churches from political manipulation. Like most German Christians he espoused a traditional brand of Christian anti-Semitism, believing the Jewish people were to be condemned for their rejection of Christ. Though he failed to recognize the terrible danger of such a position, he was at the same time strongly opposed to the Nazi condemnation of the Jews on the basis of "race."

The conflict became clear when anti-Jewish legislation was applied even to baptized Christian pastors of "non-Aryan" extraction. Niemoeller believed that to acquiesce in such measures would spell the death of the church. In response he helped organize a petition that collected the signatures of two thousand three hundred pastors pledging their opposition to the Aryan laws. The Pastor's Emergency Committee that Niemoeller founded later fed into the so-called Confessing Church, in which Karl Barth and Dietrich Bonhoeffer were also prominent. This movement was founded in 1934 to protest the capitulation of the churches to National Socialism. Its proponents named their historical situation to be a moment of "confession" which called into question the very identity of the true church. Ultimately, the question for Christians was "Which God do we worship: Christ or Hitler?" Within a few years, the Confessing Church would be suppressed, its members having either capitulated, or ended up in prison, in exile, or dead.

Niemoeller was arrested on July 1, 1937. In the relative political space which still existed in those days church bells throughout the country rang in protest. He was charged, among other things, with having "caused unrest among the people" by urging "rebellion against the laws and ordinances of the state." Though he was convicted, the judges could not bring themselves to sentence the war hero to prison. To this, Hitler reacted with fury, dismissing the judges and insisting that Niemoeller be remanded to a concentration camp as his "personal prisoner." Thus he was sent to the Sachsenhausen concentration camp north of Berlin. After the outbreak of war he was transferred to Dachau, where he remained until his liberation by Allied troops in 1945.

Niemoeller survived the war with his basic sense of patriotism intact. But as he gradually learned the extent of Nazi crimes, his attitude changed. Despite his own sufferings, he refused to evade responsibility. While his arrest in 1937 provided an "alibi" for the subsequent years, there was no such excuse, he claimed, for his failure to speak out as effectively as he might have in earlier years – especially on behalf of the Jews. In the sufferings of all who had been persecuted during those years God in Jesus Christ had been saying to him, "Are you prepared to save me?" Sadly, he admitted, "I turned that service down."

Thus Niemoeller parted company with the many Germans who refused to acknowledge any responsibility for the Nazi atrocities. He helped draft a confession of guilt for the churches which emphasized in particular the Christian role in fostering and tolerating a climate of anti-Semitism.

But this was not the end of Niemoeller's conversion. For years after the war he had maintained a sense of pride in his record of military service. But his attitude toward war began to change after the dropping of the atomic bomb. When he later learned of the immense destructive power of the hydrogen bomb, he went home, reread the Sermon on the Mount, and declared that he could no longer justify the use of force. As he described the key to his ethical principles, he said it was easy. In every situation he simply asked the question, "What would Jesus do?"

In the 1950s and in subsequent decades he became a prominent figure in the international pacifist movement, traveling the world to speak out against the perils of nuclear war and bearing witness to the cause of peace and human rights. He continued his activity until he was past the age of ninety. Born on January 14, 1892, he died peacefully on March 5, 1984.

There is always a danger in speaking out against evil, and Martin Niemoeller took the risks and the danger. It is also very difficult to admit that we have been wrong and to change our behavior. Do you find it difficult to admit that you have been wrong? Is there anything in your life and behavior that should be changed? Have you ever admitted that you were wrong about something? Was it difficult? Explain.

CHAPTER 19

The Sign of Jonah

I asked for strength that I might achieve:

I was made weak that I might humbly obey.

I asked for health that I might do greater things:

I was given infirmity that I might do better things.

I asked for riches that I might be happy:

I was given poverty that I might be wise.

I asked for power that I might have the praise of men:

I was given weakness that I might feel the need of
    God.

I got nothing I asked for,

But everything I hoped for.

I am among all men the most richly blessed.

– FROM THE JOURNAL OF A CONFEDERATE SOLDIER

Jonah was angry because he had been sent to the Ninevites to warn them that their sins were crying to heaven and that punishment was imminent. He knew that God was gracious and forgiving and that, if the Ninevites repented and changed their ways, God would show mercy to them. And that is exactly what happened. The Ninevites, from the king to the humblest citizen, repented of their evil ways and did penance for their sins, and God relented.

"I know that You are a gracious God and merciful, slow to anger, and abounding in *hessed,* Who hesitates to punish." And then Jonah complained, "Did I not say before I left my own country that this would happen… That is why I did not want to go when you sent me." The prophet thought his efforts were useless because God did not punish the Ninevites. But God told him that He had more stake in the people of Nineveh than Jonah, who had spent only a few days there. "I am their Creator and I love them. Stop complaining."

Good people often think they have a corner on God's love and mercy, but God is constantly telling us about "the sign of Jonah." His prophets should rejoice when their words are listened to and not think their time is wasted if God shows mercy to the sinners.

Jesus carried this lesson further with His story of the Good Shepherd, who went in search of the lost sheep, lifted him onto his shoulders, and carried him back to the fold. God goes after His lost sheep, and there is more joy in heaven over one sinner who repents than for ninety-nine others who have no need of repentance. In the Parable of the Prodigal Son, the son who wasted his inheritance in evil living was received back when he returned home. Like the older son in this story, some good people think God is unfair.

CATHERINE DE HUECK DOHERTY

Catherine Kolyschkine, as she was first named, was born in Russia on the feast of the Assumption in 1896. Her father, a wealthy diplomat and industrialist, was half Polish and Catholic, and so Catherine was raised in the Catholic church. When she was fifteen she married Baron Boris de Hueck, which made her a baroness. No sooner had she made this entry into the aristocracy than Russia was plunged into the First World War. While the baron served as an officer on the front, Catherine worked as a nurse. They watched as the starving and demoralized Russian army began to retreat, presaging a collapse of the tsarist empire in the October Revolution of 1917.

Though Catherine and Boris were reunited, their situation, as aristocrats, was perilous. Deprived of food rations, they came close to starving before risking a hazardous flight across the border to Finland. By 1920 they had arrived with their newborn son in Canada. Still in desperate financial straits, Catherine traveled to New York in search of work. She held a number of low-paying jobs. Finally, while working as a department store sales clerk, she was approached by a woman who asked if it were true that she was a Russian baroness, and would she be interested in lecturing about her experiences. Catherine immediately agreed, and soon she was on the lecture circuit, making $300 a week describing her harrowing escape from communism. During this time her marriage collapsed. It seemed that she had finally put the memory of poverty and hunger behind her. She had a luxurious apartment, a fancy car, and a country house in Graymore – all that communism had taken away from her. And yet her conscience was clouded by a nagging doubt, a feeling that it was just such a materialistic life and the failure of Christian values that had fed the communist revolution.

At the peak of her success she felt the pull of the gospel verse, "Go, sell what you have and give to the poor. Then come follow me." So in 1930 she gave up her worldly goods and moved into an apartment in the slums of Toronto, committed to living "the gospel without compromise." With the support of the archbishop, she came to establish the Friendship House, a storefront center for works of mercy, where the hungry were fed and the homeless were welcomed. Catherine's program of action was simple and unsystematic. It was simply a matter of living among the poor with an open door and an open heart. There was no need to seek out people in need. They came to her.

She received encouragement in these years from Dorothy Day, whose Catholic Worker movement was operating on similar principles in New York's Bowery. In 1937 Catherine herself moved to New York to establish a Friendship House in Harlem. She had come to feel that the sin of racial prejudice and the consequent segregation of whites and blacks was the greatest countersign to the gospel. Friendship House was a sign of interracial justice and reconciliation.

Among those moved by her example was the young Thomas Merton, who heard Catherine speak in 1938 and who joined her for a time in Harlem. Years later, in his autobiography, he described her message:

"Catholics are worried about Communism: and they have a right to be... But few Catholics stop to think that Communism would make very little progress in the world, or none at all, if Catholics really lived up to their obligations, and really did the things Christ came on earth to teach them to do: that is, if they really loved one another, and saw Christ in one another, and lived as saints, and did something to win justice for the poor."

Catherine was a large woman whose bearing of authority, commanding presence, and thick Russian accent seemed appropriate to the title of Baroness. That is indeed how most people addressed her. But to her friends she was simply "the B." She was famous for her earthy humor and her righteous anger. When a society woman sniffed contemptuously, "You smell of the Negro," Catherine retorted, "And you stink of hell!"

Nevertheless, her imperious style of leadership led to tensions. In 1946 Catherine resigned from Friendship House. By this time she had married a famous journalist, Eddie Doherty. Together they moved back to Ontario, Canada, and settled on a piece of land in the forest of Combermere. Catherine established a new community called Madonna House, which became a place of prayer and retreat. At Madonna House she returned full circle to the atmosphere of Russian spirituality she had known in her youth. Out of this came her best-selling book, *Poustinia*. The "poustinia," the Russian word for desert, is a place of silence and withdrawal from the compulsions of the world, a place to listen to God. It could be a hut in the forest, a special room in our apartment, or even a special place within our hearts, to which from time to time we might retreat. Through Madonna House and the communities it inspired around the world, Catherine promoted the two principles by which she lived – a commitment to the social apostolate in the world and the need to root such a commitment in a life of prayer and the spirit of Christ.

She died on December 14, 1985.

What did Catherine mean by saying she wanted to live "the gospel without compromise"? Describe how she did this. How could you begin to live the gospel while being rooted in prayer?

Love God, Love Your Neighbor

Father in heaven,

the perfection of justice is found in Your love,

and all mankind is in need of Your Law.

Help us to find this love in each other,

that justice may be attained

through obedience to Your Law.

– FROM THE SACRAMENTARY IN ORDINARY TIME

The prophets tried to turn water into wine: the water of disobedience and selfishness into the wine of fidelity and kindness. They pointed out with fire and steel the transgressions of God's people and made it clear that they are loved precisely because they are God's people.

It seems that when people turn away from God, they become brutal and merciless to others. That is why God commanded us: "You shall love the Lord, your God, and your neighbor as yourself." When these two commandments are set aside, human relationships wither and a potential friend becomes an enemy instead. Look at the world around you: Where are the places of violence? Where is there hatred, cruelty, and senseless feuds? These are the first things the prophets tackled, and it is clear that no one wanted to listen to them. "Do not carry on so," the prophet Micah was told. "No one should preach such things. Disgrace will not overtake us."

His first words were for the leaders of the people: "You are the ones who ought to know right – you who hate the good and love evil, who tear the skin off my people, and their flesh off their bones; who eat the flesh of my people, and flay the skin from them."

Four hundred years had passed since the death of David, and his kingdom was cut in two. The memory of David's fidelity to God was distant, and the people had forgotten their God and the covenant that He made with their fathers. Micah prophesied terrible things for this infidelity.

> The Lord is coming forth out of His place,
>
> And will come down and tread upon the heights.
>
> The mountains will melt under Him,
>
> And the valley will be torn open,
>
> Like wax before the fire,
>
> Like water pouring down a slope.
>
> All this because of the crime of Jacob,
>
> The sin of the House of Israel…

Zion will be plowed like a field,

Jerusalem will become a heap of ruins,

And the temple mount, a wooded height.

– Micah 1:3-5, 3:12

Prophets appear to be lonely people. Their standards are too high, their moral demands too great, and their concern too intense for others to share. Prophets often have no company except God, for they speak in the name of God.

But together with the word of warning, (the whole city and country would be taken as exiles to Babylon), Micah proclaimed the vision of redemption. Among the insights of Micah was how to accept and bear the displeasure of God. The strength of bearing this displeasure comes from the certainty that, though we have sinned against Him, He will not abandon us forever. There is compassion in His anger; when we fall, we rise. We may sit in the darkness for a while, but God is our light.

"With what shall I come before the Lord,

And bow myself before God on high?...

He has shown you, O man, what is good;

And what does the Lord require of you

But to do justice, and to love kindness,

And walk humbly with your God?"

– Micah 6:6, 8

Do you think the demands of God are too high? Why or why not? Why does God require fidelity to His command-

ments and kindness to others? What would the world be like
if those commandments were kept?

THE SWORD OF WOOD

There was once a king who loved nothing better than
to go alone at night in the clothes of a commoner: He
wanted to meet the ordinary people of his kingdom – to
learn their way of life and especially their way of thinking about the world.

One night this king found himself walking in the
poorest, narrowest street of the city. This was the street
of the Jews. He heard a song in the distance. The king
thought, *A song sung in this place of poverty must be a
lament.* But as he got closer, he could hear the true
character of the song; it was a song of pride! "Bai-yum-
dum, bai-yum-bai, yum-bai, bai…"

The king was drawn to the source of the song: the
smallest, humblest shack on the street. He knocked on
the door. "Is a stranger welcome here?"

The voice from within said, "A stranger is God's gift.
Come in."

In the dim light inside, the king saw a man sitting on
his only piece of furniture, a wooden box. When the
king came in, the man stood up and sat on the floor,
offering the king the crate for a seat.

"Well, my friend," the king asked, "what do you do to
earn a living?"

"Oh, I am a cobbler."

"You have a shop where you make shoes?"

"Oh, no, I could not afford a shop. I take my box of tools – you are sitting on them – to the side of the road. There I repair shoes for people as they need them."

"You cobble shoes by the side of the road? Can you make enough money that way?"

The cobbler spoke with humility and pride: "Every day I make just enough money to buy food for that day."

"Just enough for one day? Aren't you afraid that one day you won't make enough and then you'll go hungry?"

"Blessed be the One who carries us day by day."

The next day the king determined to put this man's philosophy to the test. He passed a proclamation that anyone wishing to cobble shoes by the side of the road must purchase a license for fifty pieces of gold.

That night the king returned to the street of the Jews. Again he heard a song in the distance, and thought, *This time, the cobbler will be singing a different tune.* But when the king neared the house, he heard the cobbler sing the same song. In fact, it was even longer, with a new phrase that soared joyfully: "Ah, ha-ah-ah, ah-ha, ah-yai."

The king knocked on the door. "Oh, my friend, I heard about that wicked king and his proclamation. I was so worried about you. Were you able to eat today?"

"Oh, I was angry when I heard I could not make my living in the way I always have. But I knew I am entitled to make a living, and I will find a way. As I stood there, saying those very words to myself, a group of people passed me by. When I asked them where they were going, they told me: into the forest to gather firewood. Every day they bring back wood to sell as kindling. When I asked them if I could join them, they said, 'There is a whole forest out there. Come along!'"

"So I gathered firewood. At the end of the day I was able to sell it for just enough money to buy food for today."

The king sputtered. "Just enough for one day? What about tomorrow? What about next week?"

"Blessed be the One who carries us day by day."

The next day the king again returned to his throne and issued a new proclamation that anyone caught gathering firewood in the royal forest would be inducted into the royal guard. For good measure he issued another: No new members of the royal guard would be paid for forty days.

That night the king returned to the street of the Jews. Amazed, he heard the same song! But now it had a third part that was militant and determined: "Dee, dee, dee, dee-dee, dee-dee, da…"

The king knocked on the door. "Cobbler, what happened to you today?"

"They made me stand at attention all day in the royal guard. They issued me a sword and a scabbard. But then they told me I wouldn't be paid for forty days."

"Oh, my friend, I bet you wish now that you had saved some money."

"Well, let me tell you what I did. At the end of the day I looked at that metal sword blade. I thought to myself. *That must be valuable.* So I removed the blade from the handle and fashioned another blade of wood. When the sword is in the scabbard, no one can tell the difference. I took the metal blade to a pawnbroker, and I pawned it for just enough money to buy food for one day."

The king was stunned. "But what if there's a sword inspection tomorrow?"

"Blessed be the One who carries us day by day."

The next day the cobbler was pulled out of line in the king's guard and was presented with a prisoner in chains.

"Cobbler, this man has committed a horrible crime. You are to take him to the square. Using your sword, you are to behead him."

"Behead him? I am an observant Jew. I couldn't take another human life."

"If you do not, we'll kill both of you."

The cobbler led the trembling man into the square, where a crowd had gathered to watch the execution, and put the prisoner's head on the chopping block. He stood tall, his hand on the handle of his sword. Facing the crowd, he spoke.

"Let God be my witness: I am no murderer! If this man is guilty as charged, let my sword be as always. But if he is innocent, let my sword turn to wood!"

He pulled his sword. The people gasped when they saw the wooden blade, and they bowed down at the great miracle that had taken place there.

The king, who had been watching all of this, came over to the cobbler. He took him by the hand and looked him deep in the eyes. "I am the king. And I am also your friend who has visited you these last several nights. I want you to come live with me in the palace and be my advisor. Please teach me how to live as you do – one day at a time."

Then, in front of everyone, the two of them danced and sang: "Bai-yum-dum, bai-yum-bai, yum-bai, bai..."

How is this story like the prophecies of Micah? What does it mean to be an observant Jew? What does it mean, "Blessed be the One who carries us day by day?"

CROESUS

Some thousands of years ago, there lived in Asia a king whose name was Croesus. The country over which he ruled was not very large, but its people were prosperous and famed for their wealth. Croesus himself was said to be the richest man in the world, and so well known is his name that, to this day, it is not uncommon to say of a very wealthy person that he is "as rich as Croesus."

King Croesus had everything that could make him happy – lands and houses and slaves, fine clothing to wear, and beautiful things to look at. He could not think of anything that he needed to make him more comfortable or contented. "I am the happiest man in the world," he said.

It happened one summer that a great man from across the sea was traveling in Asia. The name of this man was Solon, and he was the lawmaker of Athens in Greece. He was noted for his wisdom and, centuries after his death, the highest praise that could be given to a learned man was to say, "He is as wise as Solon."

Solon had heard of Croesus, and so one day he visited him in his beautiful palace. Croesus was now happier and prouder than ever before, for the wisest man in the world was his guest. He led Solon through his palace and showed him the grand rooms, the fine carpets, the soft couches, the rich furniture, the pictures, the books. Then he invited him out to see his gardens and his orchards, and his stables, and he showed him thousands of rare and beautiful things that he had collected from all parts of the world.

In the evening as the wisest of men and the richest of men were dining together, the king said to his guest, "Tell me now, O Solon, who do you think is the happiest of all men?" He expected that Solon would say, "Croesus."

The wise man was silent for a moment, and then he said, "I have in mind a poor man who once lived in Athens and whose name was Tellus. He, I doubt not, was the happiest of all men."

This was not the answer that Croesus wanted, but he hid his disappointment and asked, "Why do you think so?"

"Because," answered his guest, "Tellus was an honest man who labored hard for many years to bring up his children and to give them a good education. And when they were grown and able to do for themselves, he joined the Athenian army and gave his life bravely for the defense of his country. Can you think of anyone who is more deserving of happiness?"

"Perhaps not," answered Croesus, half choking with disappointment. "But who do you think ranks next to Tellus in happiness?" He was quite sure now that Solon would say, "Croesus."

"I have in mind," said Solon, "two young men whom I knew in Greece. Their father died when they were mere children, and they were very poor. But they worked manfully to keep the house together and to support their mother, who was in feeble health. Year after year they toiled, nor thought of anything but their mother's comfort. When at length she died, they gave all their love to Athens, their native city, and nobly served her as long as they lived."

Then Croesus was angry. "Why is it," he asked, "that you make me of no account and think my wealth and power are nothing? Why is it that you place these poor working people above the richest king in the world?"

"O king," said Solon, "no man can say whether you are happy or not until you die. For no man knows what misfortunes may overtake you, or what misery may be yours in place of all this splendor."

Many years after this there arose in Asia a powerful king whose name was Cyrus. At the head of a great army, he marched from one country to another, overthrowing many a kingdom and attaching it to his great empire of Babylonia. King Croesus with all his wealth was not able to stand against this mighty warrior. He resisted as long as he could. Then his city was taken, his beautiful palace was burned, his orchards and gardens were destroyed, his treasures were carried away, and he himself was made prisoner.

"The stubbornness of this man Croesus," said King Cyrus, "has caused us much trouble and the loss of many good soldiers. Take him and make an example of him for other petty kings who may dare to stand in our way."

Thereupon the soldiers seized Croesus and dragged him to the marketplace, handling him pretty roughly all the time. Then they built up a great pile of dry sticks and timber taken from the ruins of his once beautiful palace. When this was finished they tied the unhappy king in the midst of it, and one ran for a torch to set it on fire.

"Now we shall have a merry blaze," said the savage fellows. "What good can all his wealth do him now?"

As poor Croesus, bruised and bleeding, lay upon the pyre without a friend to soothe his misery, he thought of the words that Solon had spoken to him years before. "No man can say whether you are happy or not until you die," and he moaned, "O Solon! O Solon! Solon!"

It so happened that Cyrus was riding by at that very moment and heard his moans. "What does he say?" he asked of the soldiers.

"He says, "Solon, Solon, Solon!" answered one.

Then the king rode nearer and asked Croesus, "Why do you call on the name of Solon?"

Croesus was silent at first. But after Cyrus had repeated his question kindly, he told all about Solon's visit at his palace and what he had said.

The story affected Cyrus deeply. He thought of the words, "No man knows what misfortunes may overtake you, or what misery may be yours in place of all this splendor." And he wondered if sometime he, too, would lose all his power and be helpless in the hands of his enemies.

"After all," said he, "ought not men to be merciful and kind to those who are in distress? I will do to Croesus as I would have others do to me." And he caused Croesus to be given his freedom, and ever afterward treated him as one of his most honored friends.

Solon was a prophet to Croesus, who, in turn, was a prophet to Cyrus. A great misfortune was changed to good by the words of a wise man. Have you ever acted like a prophet to anyone? Describe what you said and why.

Hope and Healing

Our God and God of our fathers,

We thank You for teaching us

How to save others and ourselves,

To give and to receive,

And to support each other on life's journey.

There is no limit to our ascent,

For there is no limit to the goodness we can do.

There is no joy we cannot have,

There is no end to giving.

There is no height we cannot attain,

For we were created to need each other's love

And understanding.

– LIONEL BLUE

The prophet Joel was moved to prophesy when he saw a plague of locusts descending on the country. It became for him an image of God's judgment upon the people and the priests of Israel. He used the imagery of the locust plague as the basis for his prophetic exhortations for the people to repent.

Like the other prophets, Joel was appalled at the turning away from God by both the people and their leaders. As in the plague of locusts, he saw the judgment of God about to descend. "Let everybody in the country tremble, for the day of the Lord is coming, yes, it is near. Day of darkness and gloom, day of cloud and blackness…"

Joel also spoke words of comfort, hope, and promise similar to the other prophets. Good things would come to them, not from the powers and prosperity of this world or from alliances with godless nations, but from the God who loves them and watches over them.

> "I shall send you
> wheat, wine and olive oil
> until you have enough…
> Sons of Zion, be glad,
> Rejoice in the Lord your God;
> for He has given you
> autumn rains as justice demands,
> and He will send down the rains for you,
> the autumn and spring rain as of old.
>
> "The threshing floors will be full of grain,
> and vats overflow with wine and oil.

"I will make up to you for the years
devoured by locusts…
You will eat to your heart's content
and praise the name of the Lord your God
who has treated you so wonderfully."

– JOEL 2:19, 23-34, 25, 26

Repentance from evil was not a cause for grief; on the contrary, as the people returned to God, they were told, "Today is sacred to the Lord your God. Do not be mournful, do not weep… Go, eat what is rich, drink what is sweet…for today is sacred to our Lord. Do not be sad; the joy of the Lord is your stronghold."

The same is true of us when we listen to the voice of conscience, decency and kindness, the prophetic voice that we all have inside us. The day of turning back, of changing our behavior, is not a time for sadness, but for rejoicing, for the goodness of God has entered our hearts, and there is nothing to fear. That is the message of the prophets: Turn away from evil and do good, and the blessing of your God will descend upon you.

The prophet Joel saw the judgment of God in the form of a plague of locusts. Are there other images that could be used? In the story of the Prodigal Son, Jesus used another image. Do you remember what it was?

Repentance is a word that is not used much in the secular world. What does it mean? Why is it important?

CAMILLUS DE LELLIS

The mother of Camillus was sixty at the time of his birth. Since his conception was nothing short of a miracle she felt it was fit that his delivery should be similarly blessed. Thus, when she went into labor during Mass, she hurried to a stable so her son, like his Savior, could be born on a bed of straw. Such a child, she believed, was destined to be a saint.

After such an auspicious beginning, it is somewhat ironic to encounter the future saint some twenty years hence, a towering man (six-foot-six), a soldier of fortune with an irascible temper, a penchant for brawling, and a serious addiction to gambling. Camillus seems to have inherited these qualities from his father, an old soldier, considerably less pious than his wife. Together father and son went off to fight the Turks with the Venetian army. In the course of these adventures Camillus developed a hideous and painful sore on his leg, which would afflict him for the rest of his life. He was sent to the hospital of San Giacomo in Rome, where he worked as a servant while also undergoing treatment. His nursing talents were appreciated, but his temper was so intolerable that he was dismissed to return to the army.

Soon his physical suffering was compounded by the consequences of his own temperament. His gambling resulted in his losing everything, including the proverbial shirt off his back. In desperation he took a job as a builder for a Capuchin community. There his exposure to the friars awakened a dormant thirst for God and he vowed to amend his life. He sought to enter a religious community, but his ailment proved an impediment. (Sound health was required for entrants to religious orders.) Instead he returned to San Giacomo and devoted himself, in a spirit of religious discipline, to the care of the sick and dying.

Charity was not a virtue commonly associated with hospitals at the time, and healing was virtually as rare. Conditions in San Giacomo, as in most other hospitals, were appalling. Aside from the filth, the care provided by indifferent and even sadistic staff members – often recruited from the criminal class – was often more insidious than any illness. In this environment Camillus was determined to infuse an atmosphere of love. In the spirit of his newfound faith he sought to treat each sick and dying person as another Christ, a living sacrament. Before long his loving ministrations, combined with his appreciation for the value of good nutrition, cleanliness, and fresh air, produced results that appeared miraculous. The administrators of the hospital elevated him to the position of superintendent.

By this time, however, Camillus had conceived the idea of an association of similarly minded nurses, for whom the care of the sick and dying would be a religious discipline. His confessor, Philip Neri, encouraged him to proceed with this project. He also suggested that Camillus might be able to add the comforts of the sacraments to his nursing care should he become a priest.

And so Camillus dutifully applied himself to the study of Latin and theology and received holy orders in 1584.

Soon after this he left San Giacomo with two other companions to establish a model hospital in Rome. In 1591 Pope Gregory XIV recognized Camillus and his Ministers of the Sick, allowing them to wear a religious habit adorned with a large red cross. The community grew and its members proved their mettle by volunteering for service amid outbreaks of plague. Camillus was not content to wait for the sick to come to him: He used to scour the caves and catacombs of the city to seek out any who suffered. Given the conditions under which they worked, it is no surprise that many of the ministers became sick and died.

Camillus personally founded fifteen houses of his order and eight hospitals. He himself remained in more or less unbearable pain, though to the end he insisted on providing personal care at the bedside of the most miserable cases. He eventually died in Genoa on July 14, 1614, at the age of sixty-four.

Camillus de Lellis learned the meaning of repentance the hard way. What do think it was that turned him back to God? He was a heavy drinker, a gambler, and a ruffian with a bad temper, but all of this changed. Repentance sometimes turns a bad person into someone who spends the rest of his or her life doing good to and for others. Why do you think this happens? Is there any parallel to this in your own life or in someone you know?

Acknowledgments

We would like to thank all of those who have given permission to include prayers, poems, stories, and quotes. We apologize for any inadvertent omissions that may have occurred. Every effort was made to trace ownership and obtain necessary permissions.

CHAPTER 1

"O Lord, open my eyes..." by Alan Paton, from *2000 Years of Prayer.* Copyright © 1999 Michael Counsell. By permission of Morehouse Publishing, Harrisburg, Pennsylvania.

Excerpts from *The Prophets* by Abraham Joshua Heschel. Copyright © 1962 Harper & Row.

"Harriet Tubman: Abolitionist" from *All Saints: Daily Reflections on Saints, Prophets, and Witnesses for Our Time.* Copyright © 1999 Robert J. Ellsberg. By permission of The Crossroads Publishing Company.

"Mouthpiece of God" by Christina Rossetti, from *The Doubleday Prayer Collection,* selected and arranged by Mary Batchelor, Doubleday, 1997.

"Bartolomé de Las Casas: Defender of the Indians" from *All Saints: Daily Reflections on Saints, Prophets, and Witnesses for Our Time.* Copyright © 1999 Robert J. Ellsberg. By permission of The Crossroads Publishing Company.

Helen Keller quote from *Teacher: Anne Sullivan Macy,* by Helen Keller, Doubleday and Company, Inc., Garden City, New York, 1955.

CHAPTER 2

"Here I am, Lord..." by Michael Quoist, from *The Doubleday Prayer Collection* selected and arranged by Mary Batchelor, Doubleday, 1997.

"Fannie Lou Hamer: Prophet of Freedom" from *All Saints: Daily Reflections on Saints, Prophets, and Witnesses for Our Time.* Copyright © 1999 Robert J. Ellsberg. By permission of The Crossroads Publishing Company.

"Seattle: Chief of the Suquamish" from *All Saints: Daily Reflections on Saints, Prophets, and Witnesses for Our Time.* Copyright © 1999 Robert J. Ellsberg. By permission of The Crossroads Publishing Company.

CHAPTER 3

"The Sleeping Sentinel" by Albert Blaisdell and Francis Ball, from *The Moral Compass.* Copyright © 1993 William J. Bennett. By permission of Simon & Schuster, New York, NY.

"John Howard Griffin: Author of *Black Like Me*" from *All Saints: Daily Reflections on Saints, Prophets, and Witnesses for Our Time.* Copyright © 1999 Robert J. Ellsberg. By permission of The Crossroads Publishing Company.

CHAPTER 4

"Diamonds and Toads" retold by Charles Perrault, from *The Book of Virtues.* Copyright © 1993 William J. Bennett. By permission of Simon & Schuster, New York, NY.

"Arthur Ashe" reprinted from *The New York Times,* February 9, 1993. Copyright © 1993.

CHAPTER 5

"Lord, I'm so glad..." by Ruth Harms Calkin, from *The Doubleday Prayer Collection* selected and arranged by Mary Batchelor, Doubleday, 1997.

"The Man Who Moved the Earth" from *The Moral Compass.* Copyright © 1993 William J. Bennett. By permission of Simon & Schuster, New York, NY.

"Sorrow" by Katherine Mansfield, 1927. By permission of The Society of Authors as the Literary Representative of the Estate of Katherine Mansfield.

"John Leary: Peacemaker" from *All Saints: Daily Reflections on Saints, Prophets, and Witnesses for Our Time.* Copyright © 1999 Robert J. Ellsberg. By permission of The Crossroads Publishing Company.

CHAPTER 6

"Oh Lord..." by David Head from *2000 Years of Prayer.* Copyright © 1999 Michael Counsell. By permission of Morehouse Publishing, Harrisburg, Pennsylvania.

"The Pig Brother" by Laura E. Richard, from *The Moral Compass.* Copyright © 1993 William J. Bennett. By permission of Simon & Schuster, New York, NY.

"The Prince's Happy Heart" from *The Moral Compass.* Copyright © 1993 William J. Bennett. By permission of Simon & Schuster, New York, NY.

CHAPTER 7

"May your Spirit guide my mind..." by Johann Freylinghausen, from *2000 Years of Prayer.* Copyright © 1999 Michael Counsell. By permission of Morehouse Publishing, Harrisburg, Pennsylvania.

"Chico Mendes: Rubber Worker and Martyr" from *All Saints: Daily Reflections on Saints, Prophets, and Witnesses for Our Time.* Copyright © 1999 Robert J. Ellsberg. By permission of The Crossroads Publishing Company.

"Abraham Lincoln's Last Day" from *John Brown's Body,* by Stephen Vincent Benet.

CHAPTER 8

"Oh God, animate us to cheerfulness…" by William Ellery Channing, from *The Doubleday Prayer Collection* selected and arranged by Mary Batchelor, Doubleday, 1997.

"Hans and Sophie Scholl: Martyrs of the White Rose" from *All Saints: Daily Reflections on Saints, Prophets, and Witnesses for Our Time.* Copyright © 1999 Robert J. Ellsberg. By permission of The Crossroads Publishing Company.

"Anne Hutchinson: Puritan Prophet" from *All Saints: Daily Reflections on Saints, Prophets, and Witnesses for Our Time.* Copyright © 1999 Robert J. Ellsberg. By permission of The Crossroads Publishing Company.

"Jerzy Popieluszko: Priest and Martyr of Solidarity" from *All Saints: Daily Reflections on Saints, Prophets, and Witnesses for Our Time.* Copyright © 1999 Robert J. Ellsberg. By permission of The Crossroads Publishing Company.

CHAPTER 9

"May the lights come…," a Celtic Prayer, from The *Doubleday Prayer Collection* selected and arranged by Mary Batchelor, Doubleday, 1997.

"Elizabeth Fry: Quaker Reformer" from *All Saints: Daily Reflections on Saints, Prophets, and Witnesses for Our Time.* Copyright © 1999 Robert J. Ellsberg. By permission of The Crossroads Publishing Company.

CHAPTER 10

"The Man Without a Country" from *The Moral Compass.*
Copyright © 1993 William J. Bennett. By permission of Simon
& Schuster, New York, NY.

"Tarpeia" retold by Sara Cone Bryant, from *The Moral Compass.*
Copyright © 1993 William J. Bennett. By permission of Simon
& Schuster, New York, NY.

CHAPTER 11

"Give me good digestion, Lord…" by Sir Thomas Merton, from
The Doubleday Prayer Collection selected and arranged by
Mary Batchelor, Doubleday, 1997.

"For My Brother Reported Missing in Action" by Thomas Merton,
from *The Collected Poems of Thomas Merton,* Copyright ©
1948 by New Directions Publishing Corp., 1977 by The
Trustees of the Merton Legacy Trust. Reprinted by permission
of New Directions Publishing Corp.

CHAPTER 12

"The Martyred Children of Birmingham" reprinted by arrange-
ment with The Heirs to the Estate of Martin Luther King, Jr.,
c/o Writers House, Inc. as agent for the proprietor. Copyright ©
Martin Luther King Jr., renewed 1991 by Coretta Scott King.

CHAPTER 13

"Lord, lift me up…" by James Matthews, from *The Doubleday
Prayer Collection* selected and arranged by Mary Batchelor,
Doubleday, 1997.

Helen Keller quote from *Teacher: Anne Sullivan Macy,* by Helen
Keller, Doubleday and Company, Inc., Garden City, New York,
1955.

CHAPTER 14

"Dear Father, whom I cannot see..." by Lilian Cox, from *The Doubleday Prayer Collection* selected and arranged by Mary Batchelor, Doubleday, 1997.

"Anne Frank: Witness of the Holocaust" from *All Saints: Daily Reflections on Saints, Prophets, and Witnesses for Our Time.* Copyright © 1999 Robert J. Ellsberg. By permission of The Crossroads Publishing Company.

"Marian Anderson" reprinted from *The New York Times,* April 9, 1993. Copyright © 1993.

CHAPTER 15

"Bring to fruition, Creator God...," author unknown, from *The Doubleday Prayer Collection* selected and arranged by Mary Batchelor, Doubleday, 1997.

"Beethoven's Triumph," from *The Moral Compass.* Copyright © 1993 William J. Bennett. By permission of Simon & Schuster, New York, NY.

CHAPTER 16

"Dear God..." by Craig Adams, from *Favourite Prayers,* ed. Deborah Cassidi, 1998.

"Oscar Schindler: Righteous Gentile" from *All Saints: Daily Reflections on Saints, Prophets, and Witnesses for Our Time.* Copyright © 1999 Robert J. Ellsberg. By permission of The Crossroads Publishing Company.

"Lenny Skutnik" taken from "Instant Hero: Rescue of Woman Brings Fame" by Blaine Harden, from *The Washington Post,* January 15, 1982. Copyright © 1982.

CHAPTER 18

"Give me a candle of the spirit..." by George Appleton from *The Doubleday Prayer Collection* selected and arranged by Mary Batchelor, Doubleday, 1997.

"Martin Niemoeller: Confessing Pastor" from *All Saints: Daily Reflections on Saints, Prophets, and Witnesses for Our Time.* Copyright © 1999 Robert J. Ellsberg. By permission of The Crossroads Publishing Company.

CHAPTER 19

"I asked God for strength that I might achieve..." attributed to the journal of an unknown Confederate soldier, from *Favourite Prayers,* ed. Deborah Cassidi, 1998.

"Catherine de Hueck Doherty: Founder of Madonna House" from *All Saints: Daily Reflections on Saints, Prophets, and Witnesses for Our Time.* Copyright © 1999 Robert J. Ellsberg. By permission of The Crossroads Publishing Company.

CHAPTER 20

"The Sword of Wood," by Doug Lipman, storyteller.

"As Rich as Croesus" by James Baldwin, from *The Book of Virtues.* Copyright © 1993 William J. Bennett. By permission of Simon & Schuster, New York, NY.

CHAPTER 21

"Our God and God of our fathers..." by Rabbi Lionel Blue, from *Favourite Prayers,* ed. Deborah Cassidi, 1998.

"St. Camillus de Lellis: Founder of the Ministers of the Sick" from *All Saints: Daily Reflections on Saints, Prophets, and Witnesses for Our Time.* Copyright © 1999 Robert J. Ellsberg. By permission of The Crossroads Publishing Company.

Credits

Editing:	Lynn Holm
Acknowledgments:	Kristin Wittmann
Production:	Mary Steiner
Layout:	Anne Hughes
Cover Design:	Margie Brabec

009-19-0036